Profile of Man and Culture in Mexico

BY SAMUEL RAMOS

Translated by PETER G. EARLE

Introduction by Thomas B. Irving

Fourth Printing, 1969

Standard Book Number 292–73340–2
Library of Congress Catalog Card No. 62–9792
Copyright © 1962 by Adela Palacios Vda. de Ramos
All Rights Reserved

Manufactured in the United States of America

TRANSLATOR'S PREFACE

Almost simultaneously (in 1933 and 1934) the first editions of three significant essays on Latin-American man and culture were published. In Brazil, Gilberto Freyre's *The Masters and the Slaves*; in Argentina, Ezequiel Martínez Estrada's *X-Ray of the pampa*; in Mexico, Samuel Ramos' present work, *Profile of Man and Culture in Mexico*. All are profound and scrupulously honest expressions of a revitalized national consciousness.

Ramos begins with an analysis of Mexican mimetism in the nineteenth century, attributing that tendency to an underlying fear of inferiority. "Self-denigration" accompanied imitation, and both were the result of unfavorable comparisons of Mexico to Europe. The same sense of inferiority is the central theme of his penetrating chapter, "Psychoanalysis of the Mexican." He then proceeds to show how Mexico's cultural growth in the twentieth century is the achievement of those educators and exemplary personalities who have adapted the best of European heritage to the realities of native circumstance. "Creole culture" has become the inspiration of modern Mexico.

The author's condemnation of nationalistic vanity is not destructive. Inner misery concealed by nationalistic vanity has led empires into permanent decline, and today the annihilation of many nations—great and small—is a possible consequence of that collective psychic weakness. Ramos concludes that the whole basis for the inner misery of the Mexican nation is false. Accordingly, he asks his countrymen to dispense with delusion and thus eliminate the false premises of their inferiority complex. Universally valid, his message deserves universal attention.

The translator wishes to thank Willis and Helle Barnstone, of Wesleyan University, and Thomas B. Irving, of the University of Minnesota, for their helpful comments on the text. The late Dr. Ramos gave generously of his time in the summer of 1958 in order to clarify several problems of meaning.

P. G. E.

INTRODUCTION

In spite of, or perhaps because of, the many trials attending her emergence as a modern nation, Mexico has distinguished herself in her national struggle for human rights.

Mexico's pre-Columbian history extends far into the past and makes her, with Central America and Peru, one of the oldest civilizations in America, and older still than most of Europe. Her long travail under the colonial rule of Spain permitted her some degree of cultural enrichment from Europe, particularly in the late years which coincided with the American and French revolutions; but this rule was politically oppressive, and the masses of the underprivileged, like those of the Portuguese and Belgian colonies in Africa during this present century, were consistently neglected. Despite numerous proclamations and violent changes of administration throughout the nineteenth century, the masses did not begin to assume social and political power until the great Revolution of 1910. Not until then could individuals among these masses effectively demand recognition as a significant national factor, and more important, their rights as men.

Like Plato and Alexander Pope before him, Samuel Ramos believed that man is the measure of all things, and maintained that once man was restored to his place as the center of culture, then culture might offer us something of value and life itself would receive fuller meaning.

In *Profile of Man and Culture in Mexico*, Ramos insists that man must control the instruments of his civilization. Max Scheler, who has had notable influence throughout Latin America, declares that culture is not to prepare man *for* something but to develop his personality: to prepare things for man. Culture is for self-discovery; it exists to restore humanism to civilization; it is a function of the spirit destined to humanize reality.

Though relatively new in the Western world, Mexico has already contributed much to Western culture. The Revolution of 1910 has brought Mexico into close contact with the modern world, but her national conscience is still disturbed by the plight of the Indian and the downtrodden city dweller. Ramos' interest in modern anthropology enabled him to see clearly the causes and consequences of the common man's problem. Ramos also understood that the Mexican intellectual revival, to which he contributed inspiringly in this brief book and later in *Toward a New Humanism*, would have to incorporate the vitality of native culture into national life.

Samuel Ramos was born in 1897 in the town of Zitácuaro in the western state of Michoacán. He earned his bachelor's degree in the state capital of Morelia, and then went on to Mexico City to study in the Army medical school because he felt he should become a doctor like his father. However, young Ramos was not really interested in medicine or in the Army, so he transferred to the National University, where he was to be influenced by the noted sociologist and philosopher, Antonio Caso. At home, the elder Ramos had given his son a taste for letters, and under the triple influence of such a background, good scientific training, and a university teacher who inspired many a student to take up philosophy, Samuel Ramos soon became a distinguished professor of social philosophy and aesthetic theory, a position he filled until his death in June, 1959.

Professor Ramos developed a great interest in the application of scientific experience, especially that of modern anthropology, to the solution of present-day problems. *Profile of Man and Culture in Mexico* marks his attempt to place those findings which deal with his own country in an ordered system. It is both a psychological study of the Mexican mind and a suggestion of how Mexican culture can find its way into a harmonious pattern with the rest of the world. This may seem to have little bearing on our own way of life, but as we view Ramos' method we come across many instances in which the same diagnosis and treatment can help us meet the troubles we face in understanding other developing countries.

A double aspect of Mexican life has been the disparagement the average Mexican directs toward himself and his country, and the resulting desire to imitate whatever is foreign. Imitation was a means of negating this supposed inferiority of native culture. This attitude is the result of the peculiar conditions of a nation which has its origins in a highly developed autochthonous civilization that was later reduced to colonial status, and only gradually has been attaining cultural independence through a fusion of the Spanish and native elements in a Creole consciousness, which represents the hard core of Mexican character. However, Spanish individualism would never permit any true fusion, and, especially during the nineteenth century, the Creole and mestizo increased the complication by trying to pattern Mexican life along French and liberal lines, a virtually impossible transplantation, at least so long as the environment was not taken into consideration.

One of the gravest features of this environment is the subjection under which the colony was placed, a factor not greatly aided by the so-called "Egyptianism" of the Indian, or what Professor Earle has translated as his "immutability." The Indian lived for so many centuries under his own, and then the Spanish, master that he now has little concept of a changing world. The present-day Indian is not so much an artist as an artisan who produces articles by following a traditional routine skill. It is only when he is removed from his social milieu that the Indian combats this inaction and displays his creative qualities. The real master of the nineteenth century was the mestizo; but the mestizo erred by trying to assimilate French culture as fervently as the Indian before him had adopted the Christian saints. Consequently, the mestizo never reached his full development.

To understand the Mexican, it is necessary to psychoanalyze him. We have noticed that Mexico is at odds with herself in more than one way. As in the case of most developing societies, not all members of Mexican society are fully incorporated into the whole. Thorstein Veblen, by his comparison of the high-bred gentleman and the rowdy, has described how the lowest elements of a population mirror the weaknesses of the leisure class. Likewise, Samuel Ramos commences with the *pelado*, or city tramp, and shows how his language and manners display a preoccupation with social inferiority. He seeks salvation in what appears to be his strength: his masculinity, so that his speech is shot through with coarse sexual allusions asserting this will to power. Similarly, the Mexican in better circumstances tries to justify Mexico by calling European grapes sour: "A European says he has science, art, technique, etc.; however we have none of that, but at least we are *men!*"

Ramos calls this masculine boasting a smoke screen to cover up the distrust the Mexican feels toward himself and others. Even the middle-class Mexican feels compelled to apologize for himself and make allowances for his country. Only the Indian does not worry, has no influence, except that by his very passivity he exerts what Ramos calls a "catalytic" effect: his mere presence has forced the rest of the population to reckon with him, though he does nothing on his own.

To overcome this, the Mexican must take stock of himself, follow the Socratic (and Adlerian) admonition to "know thyself," and from this, to combat his weaknesses. Then he may realize that he has no insuperable problem, especially if he understands that wherever European standards do not apply, he has nothing to worry about. In its progression from the Franciscan fortress-churches to the rich reliefs of the national baroque so reminiscent of the ancient native stonework, architecture shows how this native adaptation of European forms could be harmoniously achieved.

The Mexican's passion for religion is manifest even in the great reform movement of 1857, which divided the country and led to the French intervention under Maximilian. This feeling opened up another cleft in the Mexican personality: the previous enthusiasm for the French Revolution during the first years of Independence culminated in the adoption of liberalism as a religious cult. As a result, science was deified, until it almost became Bacon's apotheosis of error. It also led to an idealism which is best exemplified in another fellow continental, the Uruguayan Rodó, who tried to adapt the positivism of Comte, Taine, and Spencer to this side of the Atlantic. In Mexico this inspiration gave great impulse to the liberators and reformers, but it also complicated the social tangle, for it really did not satisfy the basic religious yearning of the Mexican people.

The forerunner of the present generation of intellectuals and the torchbearer for French influence was Justo Sierra, whose *Political Evolution of the Mexican People* is still worthy of study by anyone interested in understanding Mexican national development over the centuries. After the French intrusion, he reëstablished the National University, and his teaching inspired the generation just past. This group of men included the sociologist Antonio Caso, whom we have already mentioned, the eccentric figure of José Vasconcelos, late director of the National Library, and Alfonso Reyes, diplomat, essayist, and cofounder of the Colegio de México, a vigorous new intellectual activity. During the first decade of the present century, before Díaz went out of power, these young men formed the Atheneum of Youth, which fostered the conviction that without cultural discipline both inspiration and genius were futile.

However, before the Atheneum accomplished much the Revolution of 1910 broke out, and with the agrarian movement Comte and Spencer passed from favor. Then the spiritualism of Bergson and James took their place. In 1919 Vasconcelos as Secretary of Education initiated a vast scheme of popular education, and later ran unsuccessfully for the Mexican presidency, an experience which left him a bitterly disillusioned man. The cry was for something more "useful," and ever since, Mexico has been disturbed by this strange tangling of utilitarianism and a semiracial mysticism.

Culturally Mexico had long been a colonial country, seeking her salvation from abroad. But works like Spengler's *Decline of the West* invited her to reject Europe, and men like Rivera and Orozco could seek themes from the native soil and expound them in their mural paintings. From this isolationism arose the danger that progress in Mexico might be impeded. For a Mexican to ignore his country in order to become wholly European would amount to intellectual betrayal. On the other hand, the Old World is indispensable to his evocation of a national utopia. Mexico must look for universal culture, but this universal culture must also express the national soul and will.

Recently the United States has spread a mechanistic view of life wherein man is reduced to a mere instrument, Yankee vitality making a bizarre contrast to the languor of this semitropical land with its naked men sheltered only by a bountiful climate. Ramos believed we should reconsider the function of education:

If schooling is good only for the instruction of material techniques, that means it is preparing individuals to be devoured all the more easily by civilization. This is indeed a monstrous concept of schooling. In contrast, education must be thought of as the vicar of life itself, fighting off a civilization which by converting men into foolproof automatons creates the illusion that it has adequately prepared them for life—though without will, or intelligence, or feeling. In short, without a soul.

Until recently Mexicans have not been sufficiently sincere about their history. In considering culture they have tended to overemphasize pure learning, sometimes forgetting in their enthusiasm that through culture man's spirit strives to humanize reality. If education has a proper aim, then it must not merely strive to increase knowledge, but to use knowledge in a spiritual capacity which enables us to know and elaborate the material offered by each individual experience.

Man must not be forgotten. Professor Ramos was preoccupied by the shrug with which the average Mexican dismissed humanism. The crisis in the rest of the world reveals that modern civilization has too many contradictions to be swallowed wholesale. Above all, the role of technique must be understood, as must the mind of the Indian as he faces new problems. Perhaps he is psychologically unfitted for the machine; for even though he can learn to drive a tractor, he cannot share the white man's yearning to build and control mechanical monsters. The Indian is humble, he does not care to dominate.

And perhaps he is right in thinking that if the machine does not free us ultimately, wherein lies its usefulness?

Man can no longer handle the problems he has created, and until he puts forth some solution, the meaning of the present day is lost; we are only flies caught in the web of our civilization, powerless to move toward the goals we should like to reach. Perhaps a better analogy is the ant, who many thousands of years ago ceased creating anything. But it seems at least that we have finally recognized the paradox: Man has ended by becoming the machine! People have become aware of this enigma, and a second Independence movement is needed, which will free the spirit for a happier destiny.

It might be useful to discuss Ramos' basic philosophic position at greater length. For instance, although Nicolai Hartmann evidently adds meaningfully to Ramos' philosophy of values, and Bergson's influence is suggested at almost every turn—in the significance he gives to action, his distrust of pure intellect (a typical Mexican reaction to the positivism prevalent under Porfirio Díaz), and the emphasis on "becoming" as opposed to "being," what about Unamuno? Is not some of the Spaniard's outlook reflected in Ramos? Ortega y Gasset is of course another source, for man's dehumanization by the machine is a theme made famous by Unamuno, Ortega, and perhaps most of all by Berdyaev.

Some of the answers to these questions can be found in *Toward a New Humanism*, a work he published in 1940 and which has not been translated. This book was an attempt by Ramos to state what he considered another interest for this age, which he called setting up "philosophical anthropology." He claimed that the crisis involving humanity had arisen because the philosopher had despaired of solving the problems of the real world, and as a result the man of action has attempted to solve them through purely pragmatic methods. This led to a dualism and a confusion expressed in the divorce between our theory and our action. Therefore we have lost our sense of the true values of life and find ourselves perplexed by this bifurcation between duty and expediency. Modern philosophy must reorient itself toward some solution of this dilemma.

This has been no more than a glance at one man's cabinet of ideas, but we live in a hurried age and one can only hope that this survey may give us some consolation in our own attempt to understand the world. We must all solve our problems through careful analysis of what those social phenomena are which have escaped our control, and why man has been counting for so little and the machine has been exacting so much in the way of tribute. Some form of idealism must help us meet our realities, and perhaps Samuel Ramos has given us a clue to the procedure we in turn must follow.

The Mexican of the twentieth century is thinking and acting for the collective good. He has a future. The Revolution and the period of energetic reconstruction following it have succeeded in uniting the country. The economy is different now, a combination of agriculture and industry which is becoming better and better balanced. Mexico is no longer shamming Europe, but probing her own reality. The Mexican takes new satisfaction from his national identity, as he contemplates his country's great achievements over the past quarter-century and the recent archeological discoveries which extend his history back into the millenia. University and cultural life is vigorous not only in the capital, where it has always been centered, but also throughout the state capitals and other cities. Many people have been formed in this movement, many new jobs have been opened up, and it is all symbolized in the delightful and innovating architecture found in most Mexican cities.

Mexico is on the road up, the errors of youth are giving way to the experience of maturity. Mexicans no longer need to learn how to die; they may now even plan how to live.

T. B. IRVING
University of Minnesota

CONTENTS

PROFILE OF
Man and Culture
IN MEXICO

PROLOGUE TO THE THIRD EDITION

With the publication of the third edition of this book, it seems appropriate to respond to some of the commentaries on its principal theses. Since its appearance in 1934, the book has been generally well received. The first edition was quickly sold out, and in the year 1938 a second edition appeared. Over the years the book has had wide circulation, not only in Mexico but throughout the Hispanic-American world, and has been frequently cited in a multitude of articles and books on the culture of Mexico and America. These facts show that the book opened up a new field to research and thought, one which generally speaking had scarcely been explored. Some ideas in our country which were expressed in this book—such as those concerning Mexican psychology— have become commonplaces, a fact which demonstrates their general acceptance. But one of the effects which has pleased this writer most is the stimulus and impulse which his book has given to studies on Mexican psychology and culture—whether as books on general themes or as monographs on special topics.

Since the fact that many of the themes had not been discussed before made it difficult to classify the book in one of the established scientific disciplines, it was hard to know whether to consider it as a rather impassioned critique of Mexican life, or as a serious essay on social psychology. Several years were necessary for well-informed critics to decide on a valid definition of the book: an essay on the characterology (*caracterología*) and philosophy of culture.

The basic idea of this book grew out of its author's ambition to establish a theory which would explain the real character of Mexican man and his culture. This task called for an interpretation of our history and led to the discovery of certain national vices, the knowledge of which seems to me indispensable as a point of departure for a serious undertaking of the spiritual reform of Mexico.

It never occurred to me that the vices indicated in my book were incorrigible, except in the case of people who persist in ignoring them and in relegating to the subconscious their psychological causes. If the causes are accepted as a valid general thesis, the affirmations in this book should follow as a logical consequence: any real reform in Mexican life depends first on a profound reform in the character of our people.

Some have tried to interpret one of the fundamental theses of the book—that the Mexican suffers from a sense of inferiority—as if this implied a real somatic or psychic inferiority in the Mexican race. No idea could be further from my thoughts, for I have always believed it unnecessary to presuppose a truly organic inferiority in order to explain a *sense* of inferiority. To be perfectly clear on this point, it now seems appropriate to state what I believe is the psychological mechanism that has resulted in that complex.

In the life of every man one of the most necessary feelings is that of security. It seems especially necessary when the individual has occasion to test the efficacy of his aptitudes and power. In other words: repeated success in action is what progressively instills in the individual conscience a sense of security. Favorable or adverse, exterior circumstances can undeniably have a serious effect on that sense; but whether they do or do not depends mainly on an internal factor: the degree of confidence that the individual has in himself. When a man feels that he is the complete master of his forces, he does not shrink back from the difficulties and problems that he encounters. Rather, he finds in them one more stimulus to his will, which, upon overcoming them, heightens his satisfaction in himself. It is said that every man can be successful in life, so long as he is capable of both adapting himself to the particular circumstances in which he lives and acts, and of mastering them. But one can understand that human flexibility has its limitations, and frequently there are cases in which the individual's potentiality for adaptation is not up to the demands of external circumstances. However, this does not mean that the world is closed to such individuals. In the face of such a predicament, a recourse is left which is exclusively theirs; no one need share it with anyone else, as is the case with animals. I mean to say that man has the faculty of adapting circumstances to his own needs. So, for example, he can move from place to place, until he finds what best fits his purposes; or he can abandon one occupation in order to undertake another, more in accord with his natural vocation or aptitude. Unfortunately, this full harmony between man and his working conditions does not depend simply on his intelligence or will, but also on unavoidable accidents of a social or economic order. I nevertheless believe that within the rigid restrictions that life imposes on each individual, there is a small margin of freedom in which he can decide his own acts.

Man is not a being who will readily limit himself to the bare necessities of daily life. The desire for security impels him to seek much more than the minimal requirements. There is no better way of gaining an awareness of security than by being powerful. That is why the instinct for power is a deeply rooted and vital exigency of human nature. It is therefore not surprising that numerous individuals, swept along by the urge for power, find themselves in the position of coveting much more than it is possible for them to have. Let us take the example of a person who oversteps himself in his intense ambition, and observe what happens to him spiritually when he tries to convert that ambition into reality. If the existing gap between what he wants to do and what he is able to do is great, he will undoubtedly fail, and he will suffer deep spiritual depression. Not recognizing the real error of his situation, he will look upon himself as incapable; from that moment on he will have no self-confidence; in short, a sense of inferiority will grow in his mind.

A physically sound man who strives to excel in a sport in which he has no natural ability will quite possibly suffer from an inferiority complex. We should understand that while a man's self-depreciation is absolute his inferiority is in fact only relative. This sentiment stems from a disparity between his actual resource and the goals he wants to achieve. The instinct for power carries him too far, makes impossible a frank assessment of his strength, and provokes a radical confusion between what he wants and what he is capable of. Comparing the results obtained with those he wished to obtain, he will think of himself as weak or incapable, that is, as an inferior man. But no one can live with his conscience burdened by these depressing ideas, and if the individual does not react quickly against them, he is in danger of committing suicide. Within him are strong drives toward self-preservation that tend to free him from these life-destroying notions. In certain cases it is possible for him to discover his error and correct the exaggerated idea he had concerning his personality. Then he will enter into harmony with reality, and convince himself that within a less ambitious sphere of activities he is as good as anyone else. In the light of a proper judgment of the situation, the conflict is resolved and his inferiority complex disappears. But unfortunately, not all men who overestimate their personality are prepared to abandon their flattering idea of it. There exists a psychological type of man whose fundamental purpose in life is to make his ego prevail. One can understand that the predominating instinct in such cases is the instinct for power. Love, money, culture are by comparison simply means of making his personality felt. The psychologist Jung has designated this type with the name "introvert." Such a man is disposed to everything but one basic concession which he can never make: that he is worth less than he thinks. It is precisely this mentality that constitutes the most fertile ground for development of an inferiority complex.

But in such cases how is a man to free himself from that complex, if he steadfastly maintains his false overestimation of himself? The tension created between the inferiority complex and the exalted idea of the self sometimes becomes so violent that the individual ends up with a neurosis. However, in a multitude of cases the conflict is resolved without exceeding normal limits, in such a way that the individual is satisfied, even though the solution is not beneficial to him. The only path left to him is to abandon the realm of reality and to seek refuge in fiction. If one remembers that a sense of inferiority customarily appears in childhood or adolescence—when character is beginning to take form—one can understand how the traits of that character will tend to compensate for the complex. Individuals afflicted with an inferiority complex develop a unique psychology, with unmistakable characteristics. All their attitudes tend to give them the illusion of a superiority which others do not acknowledge. Imperceptibly a fictitious personage takes the place of the authentic being, and makes the role he represents in life seem real. The individual lives a lie, but only at this price can he free his conscience from the distressing idea of his inferiority.

Here, in brief résumé, I have presented the psychological doctrine of Alfred Adler, who at first was a disciple of Freud but later followed his own course in creating a new interpretation of nervous character. Some years ago, while I was observing psychological traits common to a large group of Mexicans, it occurred to me that these traits could be explained from the point of view indicated by Adler. It is my thesis that some expressions of Mexican character are ways of compensating for an unconscious sense of inferiority. Readers who have understood my exposition of the genesis of this complex cannot infer that I attribute inferiority to Mexicans. What I maintain is that the Mexican undervalues himself, committing in this way an injustice to his person. I of course do not claim that this psychological explanation is a valid generalization for all Mexicans, for some possess other modes of character whose mechanism should be explained by other scientific principles. This means that the work is far from complete; vast regions of the Mexican soul have yet to be explored. The study is defective, among other reasons, because I found myself virtually without antecedents on which to rely; but now that the breach is open, perhaps other investigators may venture along the same road with better fortune. I shall not now repeat the ideas contained in this book. I should only like to state that I have utilized a well-known Mexican type, the *pelado*, whose conduct in compensation for his sense of inferiority corresponds, precisely, to what Adler has called "the virile protest." On the other hand, within an extensive group of individuals with members in all of the social classes, one observes character traits like distrust, aggressiveness, and hypersensitivity to insult, which undoubtedly derive from the same source.

It seems to me that the sentiment of inferiority in our race has a historical origin which must be sought in the areas of the Conquest and Colonization. But it did not really begin to manifest itself until the time of the Independence movement, when the country had to define its own national physiognomy. Being an extremely young nation, it attempted—overnight—to reach the level of traditional European civilization. It was then that the conflict broke out between ambition and the limits of natural capacity. The solution seemed to be imitation of Europe, its ideas and its institutions, creating thereby certain collective fictions which, when we have interpreted them as fact, have artificially solved our psychological conflict.

From Leonardo da Vinci comes the proverb, full of profound wisdom, "Seek what you are capable of, and be capable of what you seek." No norm of life seems more fitting for those who are victims of the illusion that their capabilities are adequate for the achievement of a seductive goal. One must not desire more than one can achieve, but first the mainspring of the will must be strained to the utmost, so that Leonardo's dictum does not degenerate into a justification of sloth or pettiness. There will always be some who think the greater a man's ambition, the better; only thus can he improve. This opinion is valid, however, only in so far as man is profoundly conscientious, and as he watches every step in order to preserve the notion of a boundary between the possible and the impossible. The Biblical maxim that "no man shall add a cubit to his height" must be kept in mind. But if the individual goes through life obsessed with the idea of superiority at all costs, and with no other purpose than to dominate others simply for the pleasure of it, then his soul will always be restless and on the defensive, and fearful that its lie will be discovered.

Mexico is a young country and youth is an ascendant force. I see in this fact the assurance that our will

strives for the elevation of man's station, for the betterment of his life, and, generally speaking, for the development of all our national capacities. I have enumerated
the vices and defects of Mexican psychology, but I am
nevertheless convinced that more favorable destinies
await us, and that the future is ours. Possibly our errors
are errors of youth, which maturity will correct. Our
psychology is that of a race in its age of fantasy and illusion; it is therefore fated to failure until it achieves a
positive sense of reality. I have faith in the salvation of
Mexico because our race lacks neither intelligence nor
vitality; it needs only to learn. However, the necessary
wisdom is not of the kind that one learns in school. It is
rather the kind that only experience can offer. I refer to
that knowledge of living which is not to be found in books
and which can be learned only in life itself. Up to now,
Mexicans have known only how to die; it is time that
they learned how to live.

I have no doubt that the majority of changes and reforms attempted in Mexico are the result of a sincere desire for improvement, and this shows the existence of
progressive inclinations. But combined with these are
other and unrecognized tendencies which weaken and
detract from their virtue. Psychoanalysis leads to a discovery in the Mexican soul of obscure forces which, dis-
guised as lofty aspirations, actually work toward an
abasement of the person. False values are often exalted
as authentic. At other times, things foreign are blindly
imitated, with the consequence that the development of
domestic potentialities is arrested. Yet occasionally those
foreign values which Mexico could use to good advantage
are rejected, under the pretext of wholesome nationalistic

purpose, even though the real reason is ineptitude. Of all these negative forces, the tendency to irrational imitation seems to dominate. Therein is expressed an impatient and childish urge to skip over preliminaries.

I have fought against the seduction of various foreign ideas and institutions because they do not answer the nation's needs and because they can counteract the higher impulses of the Mexican soul. All ideas and political regimes which seek to convert man into an animal of the herd, nullifying his freedom, every materialistic concept which considers man as a purely instinctive being, explaining his psychic functions as the effects of biological needs—whether sexual, nutritional, or simply lustful for power—all these are forces which lead to infrahumanity.

In accordance with the problem of forming the Mexican spirit the final chapter in the book presents the thesis that the ideal of our culture should be the achievement of a new humanism. Apropos of this idea, from among several commentaries arose the question about the meaning of the expression "new humanism." I felt beneath these words an insistent philosophical preoccupation with the essence of man, which called for extensive discussion, and wrote another book published under the title *Toward a New Humanism*. Clearly, the problem of the essence of man is a question of general nature which should be treated *in abstracto*, without reference to any case in particular. But even though the theme of my book *Toward a New Humanism* is considered in this way, its elaboration grew out of an idea from the preceding book; the theme is the philosophical development of this idea. So it is that the two books are interrelated, one being the consequence of the other.

The Renaissance discovered that man's hunger for existence in the hereafter reduced his attention to his present life, his mundane existence. Humanism was a spiritual movement designed to draw man from heaven back to earth, to circumscribe his thought and action within real limits, adjusted to the scope of his possibilities. Thus, humanism became a system of education which prevailed in all the schools of Europe and survives in our time in the form of the study of old languages, which convey to us the thriving life in the writings of antiquity. Through its cultural legacy—made directly intelligible by the learning of classical languages—the authentic spirit of the Greco-Latin world was discovered. It was not, however, an archeological inclination which awoke interest in the works of Greece and Rome, but the presence in these works of a living spirit of perennial significance, first becoming evident in the Renaissance. In works such as these, there existed in definitive form a sense of life similar to what then was beginning to awake within the new historical consciousness. That was the concept of life which centuries later Nietzsche would define as the "sense of the earth."

In summary one might say that while classical Humanism was a movement filtering down to earth from above, the new Humanism must work in exactly the opposite direction, that is, from the earth upward. Circumstances today demand this. In our modern civilization are a multitude of factors which have forced man down toward a level of infrahumanity. Everything which tends to hinder this descent has steadily been losing force, and the fall is accelerating, with fewer and fewer obstacles to detain it. One need be no sagacious observer to discover these traits of infrahumanity in the profile of events taking place before us. In a multitude of daily occurrences it is immediately obvious that man bears within him the will to descend to primitivism and savagery.

I.

Imitation
of Europe
in the
Nineteenth
Century

Method

Whoever aspires to a serious study of "Mexican culture" will find himself in a realm of vagueness. He will be struck by an abundance of Mexican works lacking qualities that could be said to proclaim the existence of an original, vernacular style. But the existence of unoriginal works does not mean that the nation in which they appear lacks a culture of her own. We believe that the nucleus of culture is man's way of being, even when no creative impulse lives within him. So it is that in the absence of objectivity, culture may still exist in another form: in subjectivity. A priori, then, we can neither affirm nor deny the existence of a Mexican culture. Following the Cartesian method, let us make this doubt justify the investigation we are about to undertake. Starting with the subjective concept of culture, we shall be especially concerned in our presentation with an analysis of the Mexican's psychic being.

To say what Mexican culture *is like* (supposing that it does exist), we must naturally select material that reliably represents the object of our examination. But in order to identify this object without confusing it with other similar ones, it would first be necessary to know what constitutes Mexican culture. We are in a vicious circle. To know what Mexican culture is like, we need first to grasp the meaning of our object; but we cannot grasp the meaning of our object without a previous notion of what it is like. If we seriously seek a solution to the problem of observation of purely cultural facts, without first having a definite idea of what we are seeking, we will surely end up in a blind alley.

Why not forget for the moment the question of whether Mexican culture is real, and concentrate on thinking exclusively about what such a culture *would* be like if it existed? This does not amount to placing the deductive abstraction on a different plane from that of effective realities. We know that any culture is conditioned by a certain mental structure of man, and by historical accident. When these data are ascertained, the question can then be put as follows: Given a specific human mentality and specific accidents in its history, what type of culture will that mentality acquire?

Self-Denigration

There is no basis for attributing to Mexico the existence, or even the mere possibility, of a firsthand or original culture, because it would be biologically impossible to make a *tabula rasa* of the mental constitution which history has bequeathed to us. We were not destined to enter the world isolated from all that civilization which, not being of our own making, was imposed on us as if by chance. On the contrary, there was a significant spiritual relationship. Consequently, it must be admitted that the only culture possible among us must be of a derivative kind.

Throughout its history Mexico has fed on European traditions and expressed much interest and appreciation for their value. At the time of the nineteenth-century Independence movement the most enlightend minority—in its determination to become cultured in the European fashion—comes close to divorcing itself from the nation. No one can deny that interest in foreign culture has signified for many Mexicans a spiritual flight from their own land. In this case, culture is a cloister in which men who disdain native realities take refuge in order to ignore them. From this erroneous attitude Mexican "self-denigration" was born more than a century ago, and its effects have been crucial in our historical orientation. "Spanish-American peoples," writes Carlos Pereyra in his *History of America*, "have suffered the consequences of a self-denigratory thesis maintained constantly for a century, to the extent of creating the deep-rooted sense of ethnic inferiority which a reaction can convert into an excess of vainglory." Therefore, the nation now seems justified in its reaction and sentiment against the cultural appeal of Europeanization, which it blames for the disesteem of Mexico by Mexicans themselves. Mexicans acquire still more support for their hostility to European culture when they consider the multitude of failures resulting from excessive foreign imitation.

Imitation

Popular opinion has unjustly blamed intellectual tradition for many national shortcomings. It is important to clarify this matter also, because disdain of culture can lead to consequences quite as serious as disdain of reality. The failures of culture in our country have not been due to deficiencies in the culture itself, but to a vice in the system of application. The vice in the system is none other than the *imitation* which has been universally practiced in Mexico for more than a century.

Mexicans have been imitating for a long time, without actually realizing that they were imitating. They have always sincerely believed that they were bringing civilization into national existence. Mimesis is an unconscious phenomenon that reveals a peculiar characteristic of mestizo psychology. It is not the vanity of feigning a culture that has brought about imitation. The unconscious tendency has been rather to conceal the absence of culture not only from foreign eyes but from our own. In order for something to induce imitation, belief that it is worthy of imitation is indispensable. Accordingly, our mimesis would make no sense if there were not some intuition of the value of culture.

But no sooner is this value revealed to the Mexican conscience, than the circumstantial reality—by way of comparison—is scorned, and the individual then experiences a sense of inferiority. Imitation looms forth as a psychological defense mechanism and, upon assuming a cultural appearance, it frees us from that depressing sentiment. At this point a question occurs. If the individual is able to understand culture and considers it a desirable quality, why does he not obtain it in some authentic way? He cannot, because true assimilation demands a continuous and composed effort. Since the Mexican's sense of inferiority affects his spirit and since, furthermore, his social life in the nineteenth century was at the mercy of repeated anarchy and civil war, neither composure nor continuity of effort has been possible. Whatever has to be done has to be done quickly, before some new disorder interrupts the work. On the other hand, conduct no longer obeys reflection but yields rather to the urgent impulse of curing an internal ailment. Culture from this moment loses its spiritual significance and becomes a stimulative medicine to alleviate the painful, intimate depression. When used to this therapeutic purpose, authentic culture is susceptible to substitution by its mere image.

This theory of Mexican mimesis shows that the imitation in question does not proceed from vanity; the vain person looks for the effect of his appearance on others, whereas the Mexican exploits the effect of his imitation only within himself.

There are examples of such mimesis in all orders of

culture, but the clearest ones are found in Mexican constitutional adaptations of the nineteenth century. This is the sphere in which we can best appreciate the consequences which imitation has had for Mexican history. It is therefore fitting to recall some of the more typical cases. Everyone knows that the model for our series of constitutions of the past century was taken from the United States. According to Carlos Pereyra, the first text of the United States Constitution known in Mexico was a bad translation imported by a dentist. When after the fall of the Spanish Empire a conflict between "federalism" and "centralism" arose in Mexico, Friar Servando Teresa y Mier proclaimed in a fiery oration that he would "slit his own throat" if any of his listeners knew "what breed of animal a federal republic was."

The phrase is a just criticism of the heedlessness with which modern political institutions began to be copied. Whenever some sensible voice cried out in a solitary attempt to show the discrepancy between truth and illusion, it failed to awake those dreamers. Father Mier, for example, fought against federalism for the following reasons:

Federation was a means of uniting the disunited; that is why the United States had adopted it. There, colonial history demanded a federal pact as the only possible form for the new nationality. But here it was a means of *dis*uniting the united, when everything revealed the urgency of making the brand new Mexican nation more compact, more coherent, for its population was sparsely scattered over an immense territory. If it required a somewhat decentralized administrative control, it also demanded, on the other hand, the kind of political guidance which would accelerate a cohesive movement and suppress the centrifugal tendencies of the outer regions.

By one of those accidents which often happen in Mexican history, the centralist idea became synonymous with reaction. With the triumph of liberalism our country was converted into a federal republic, though only nominally, because the pressure of reality, superior to the influence of law, forced the governments of the nineteenth century to impose on the people a feigned centralism that could maintain some degree of unity amidst the prevailing anarchy. All the principles declared by our constitutional statutes had a like fate. F. García Calderón says:

> The actual development of Ibero-American democracies, differs remarkably from the admirable spirit of their political charters. These contain all the principles of government that have been applied by the great European nations, balance of powers, natural rights, liberal suffrage, representative assemblies. But reality contradicts the idealism of these statutes imported from Europe. The traditions of the dominating race have created over-simplified and barbarous systems of government.[1]

Finally, imitation has brought about in Mexican life a situation which has not greatly attracted the attention of historians, but which is, nevertheless, essential to an understanding of our immediate past. The effect consists of an unfolding of our life on two separate planes, one real and the other fictitious. Such a disparity is perceived only by one who observes events in the perspective of time; but for the men who participated in them no difference existed between reality and fiction. When a constitution is proclaimed, for example, political reality must be appraised within its standards, but when political reality does not coincide with the constitutional precepts, it al-

[1] F. García Calderón, *Les Democraties latines de l'Amérique*, p. 341.

ways appears to be unconstitutional. The reader should
note well what we mean. If life develops in two distinct
ways—one, according to the law, and the other, according to reality—reality will inevitably be illegal; and
when in the midst of such a situation there abounds a
spirit of blind rebellion, ready to explode on the slightest
pretext, we can understand the endless chain of "revolutions" that make our nineteenth-century history a vicious
circle.

Notes for a Philosophy of Mexican History

If we try to picture the series of political
events of the past century within a logical context, we are
likely to discover that they do not make "history" at all.
Occurrences which assume historical magnitude are those
which seem determined by some basic social necessity.
The chronology of events, then, falls into an alignment
of continuous development, within which the situation
of the moment always adds a new element to the past. For
this reason, the past never reproduces itself exactly in the
present. In short, if we conceive of history as one should,
it will not appear to us in the form of a preservation of the
dead past, but in that of a living process in which the past
is transformed into an ever-new present.

Each historical moment has but one place in chronology and can never repeat itself. "In our life," observes
García Calderón with reference to all Spanish-American
history, "there is a *ricorso* that brings back on successive
revolutions the same men with the same promises and the
same methods. The same political comedy is performed
periodically: a revolution, a dictator, a program of na-

tional restoration." This periodicity in our history seems to obey an insistent intervention of the same blind, anarchic force which upsets the order of things with no other object than that of self-affirmation. When a revaluation of Mexican history is someday undertaken in the light of an improved critical consciousness of its meaning, then the monotonous narration of "*ricorsi*" will be reduced to a concise exposition of a few lines.

But such revaluation will be a marginal phenomenon, not an emanation from the profound needs of the Mexican people—whose revolution is apparent in other events which really do have historical significance. Justo Sierra says with reference to the nineteenth century:

Mexico has had only two revolutions, that is, two brusque accelerations in its evolution. They came out of that internal ferment—initiated by the milieu, race, and historical moment —which drives a nation toward the perennial realization of an ideal, and of a state superior to that in which she finds herself. . . . The first was the *Independence* or emancipation from the mother country, born of the Creoles' conviction that Spain was too impotent to govern them[2] and that they were quite capable of governing themselves. This revolution was motivated by Napoleon's attempted conquest of the Iberian Peninsula. The second revolution was the *Reform*, due to the profound need of enacting a political constitution and a liberal regime based on social transformation, on the suppression of privileged classes, on the equitable distribution of public wealth (immobilized, for the most part), on the regeneration of labor, on the vigorous development of a national conscience by means of public education. The motive for this second revolution was the North American invasion, which showed up

[2] Creoles (*criollos*) were those who in the Colonial Period were born of Spanish parents in Hispanic America. The leaders of the struggles for Mexican independence during the first twenty years of the nineteenth century were predominantly Creoles. (Translator's note)

the impotence of the privileged classes to save the fatherland, and the inconsistency of an organism that could scarcely call itself a nation. These revolutions were two historical phases of the same social effort. Freedom from Spain was the first; freedom from the colonial method of rule was the second: two stages in an identical creative functioning of the national personality in possession of itself.[3]

The vicious circle which I have mentioned constitutes, more precisely, an antihistorical element, an obstacle that has retarded the action of positive historical forces. While considering this element as primitive and unnecessary for a comprehension of our destiny, I am not unaware of its real effects. Its role in our life is comparable to that of diseases: these we can never consider as an integral part of a man's destiny, because they do not arise—as does the latter—from the deep roots of character. Nevertheless, in an accidental way they usually obstruct the march and alter the course of that destiny. Justo Sierra says:

There is no doubt that history, which in our time has scientific pretensions, should deny itself emotion and concentrate on the stability of facts, on analysis, and on coordination of its dominant characteristics, so as to achieve a synthesis. But periods abound in our history in which repetition of identical errors and identical guilt afflicts bitter and sorrowful hearts with its gloomy monotony.[4]

As for those other processes which constitute the backbone of our history, one must distinguish clearly from them the real condition that separates a movement from the ideology—usually a European assimilation—with which it disguises itself. This duality alters somewhat the profile of transcendental events of the past, events which

[3] *México y su evolución social*, I, 225.
[4] *Ibid.*, I, 200.

lose their naturalness and acquire the character of a simu-
lacrum of European history. Such is the effect of the
mimetic procedure already described. In their reliance on
principles of European civilization our compatriots are
therefore disqualified from doing spontaneous (if not creative) work in which the Mexican spirit might sincerely
speak. Perhaps the most lamentable truth of our history
(a possible result of self-denigration) is to be found in our
ancestors' feeling that they had not been themselves with
all their vices and virtues but instead had concealed reality behind a rhetorical façade from abroad. In our time
there is a fortunate tendency to correct this error by a
salutary eagerness for sincerity, which must be encouraged wherever it may appear. The foregoing observations
will give an idea of what a philosophy of Mexican history could be, were it developed in greater extent and
detail.

The Spanish Spirit in America

Near the beginning of this essay I stated
that our culture was necessarily *derivative*; but following
the observations already made, it is clear that we will not
consider as Mexican culture that which results from imitation. But is there any better method of tracing the
growth of one culture out of another? Needless to say,
there is: the important phenomenon to observe is commonly called *assimilation*. Between the processes of imitation and assimilation exists the same difference as
between the mechanical and the organic. Here also historical observation will permit us to discover—after the
most obvious application of imitation—whether any
deep-rooted assimilation of culture has taken place.

It is difficult to know to what extent one can speak of cultural assimilation. Going back to our origin, we note that through our veins runs the blood of Europeans who brought their own culture with them to America. It is true that there was a mixing, but not of cultures; because as a result of the contact between conqueror and native, the culture of the native was destroyed. In the words of Alfonso Reyes, it was "the collision of the earthenware pot with the caldron. The pot was undoubtedly very fine and beautiful, but it was obviously the more fragile."

In the evolution of our culture in America we must identify two phases: the first of *transplantation*, and the second, of *assimilation*. Not all cultures have grown by the same genetic process. Some—the oldest among them —have germinated and grown in the same soil that nourished their roots. Others—the more modern ones—have grown with the aid of foreign elements which originated in an older culture and which were grafted on. The older culture, in turn, is rejuvenated by the new blood and converted into another living form of the human spirit. In order to prove that a derivative culture exists in a given country, we must make certain that elements chosen from the originating culture have become part of the unconscious spirit of that country. By "culture" we mean not only works of disinterested, spiritual activity, but also any other form of action inspired by the spirit. From this point of view, Mexican life ever since the Colonial Era has tended to conform to the cultural molds imported from Europe. The most efficacious vehicles for this transplantation were two, language and religion. These, to be sure, were the two fundamental objectives in the educational enterprise undertaken by Spanish missionaries,

who accomplished in a most memorable feat of the sixteenth century the "spiritual conquest" of Mexico.

A certain kind of receptivity in the aboriginal race,
which was as religiously inclined as the white race that
had come to rule over it, undoubtedly made the enterprise easier. In the New World there was fertile land for
propagation of the Christian seed.

It was our fate to be conquered by a Catholic theocracy
which was struggling to isolate its people from the current of modern ideas that emanated from the Renaissance.
Scarcely had the American colonies been organized when
they were isolated against all possible heresy. Ports were
closed and trade with all countries except Spain was dis-
approved. The only civilizing agent of the New World
was the Catholic Church, which by virtue of its pedagogical monopoly shaped the American societies in a medie-
val pattern of life. Education, and the direction of social
life as well, were placed in the hands of the Church,
whose power was similar to that of a state within a state.
In probing the depths of the Spanish soul Salvador de
Madariaga finds that its essence is passion. "In Spain," he
says, "religion is first of all an individual passion like love,
jealousy, hate, and ambition." Bearing in mind the fact
that religion was experienced in this impassioned way, as
were other teachings transmitted by the Church, one can
appreciate the depth with which Catholic culture was engraved on the heart of the new race. We are calling this
culture "Creole" because it imbued the Mexican subconscious with certain traits which, if not exclusively Spanish, at least adhered to Hispanic character throughout the
colonial domination. Since the Church energetically car-
ried out this function of Spain, and since, furthermore,

the first influences on a youthful spirit are customarily the most enduring, the remains of Creole culture now represent the most rigid element of Mexican character. This was the origin of the tenacious, conservative spirit of our society. Well after the beginning of the nineteenth century, when Lucas Alamán founded the Conservative Party, he built his policy on an alliance with the Church and a return to the Spanish colonial system. The presence of that traditional culture can still be felt in the moral and religious prejudices and the routine customs of our rural middle class. But the strong resistance of traditionalism to changes demanded by time has provoked an equally vigorous reaction, one which has tended to modify the Mexican spirit along modern lines. Could the reaction have originated in some psychic element extrinsic to the Spanish part of our character? Such a theory is questionable, for the Spanish in us is not identifiable as any isolated tendency; it is rather a generic kind of reaction to be found in all our tendencies, no matter how diverse they may be. Actually, we shall find some characteristics, common to both the traditionalist and modern tendencies, which are probably hereditary manifestations of that psychological unity in which true Spanish character is condensed.

Spanish Individualism

Salvador de Madariaga's psychological theory states that as a man of passion the Spaniard inevitably rebels against any restriction imposed by collective life, and that he is consequently an individualist. Indeed, individualism is the predominant note in all phases of Spanish history. The conquest of America, for example, was not actually the work of Spain as a nation, but the achievement of individual adventurers who operated on their own initiative. Even the primitive Iberians, who lived in tribes, distinguished themselves by a great pride resistant to all forms of union and discipline. The curious thing about Spain is that there one can become an individualist to virtually any extreme and still be a Spaniard. In that country it seems that the most exalted individualists are also the most profoundly Spanish: Miguel de Unamuno is an exemplary case. The instability of Spanish life, following an ephemeral epoch of unity and imperial greatness, is the result of a centrifugal force in individuals which impedes all uniform collective action. The orientation of politics, art, literature, or ideas is determined by action of isolated personalities, sometimes without adequate correlation to prevailing realities. Each Spaniard seems to be a volatile atom, any movement of which thrusts it away from its natural center of gravity.

It appears that the independence of Spanish colonies is not explainable by the biological law which states that the young, when ready to subsist alone, can be separated from their parents. Spain's policy during her domination of America never intended that her colonies should ultimately become self-sufficient national units. But the inherent traits of Spanish character were nevertheless more powerful than the will of her successive administrations. The independence movement arose as an effect of internal, psychological causes, which were the dispersive impulses already described. "The Spaniard in America," says Madariaga, "was as individualistic as his European brother. The centrifugal force so representative of the man of passion in action revealed itself unexpectedly at the first opportunity."

Each of the colonies felt an inclination to convert itself into another Spain. Despite the fact that the revolution of independence raised its banner against Spain with the cry "Death to the gachupines!"[5] Hispanic psychology shows itself in this very same attitude of negation. We were freeing ourselves from Spain, but we were doing it *a la española.*

Influence of the Milieu

One can understand how under pressure of new social conditions—especially those of intermarriage —the Spanish characteristics of our race have undergone important modifications. We shall now attempt to find out what those modifications were.

Modern psychological doctrines teach us that it is impossible to make a man's character intelligible without knowledge of certain childhood experiences definitively influential in the evolution of his soul. We must therefore go back to the beginnings of our history, to find out whether some event could have projected the evolution of the Mexican soul into a determined orbit. There can be no doubt about the existence of such a circumstance, the exceedingly peculiar one by which Spanish American countries have entered the historical scene. At the time they were born a fully developed civilization already existed around them. Alfonso Reyes has described the situation well in saying that we were "invited to the banquet

---

[5] Gachupín, derogatory term denoting a Spaniard, often a tradesman, who resides in Mexico. It is still in wide use. (Translator's note)

of civilization after the meal had already been served."

It was impossible for the new American races to make their own way, and they failed to take advantage of the routes already established. Owing to their Spanish blood, the conquerors' descendants held a bond with Europe and —to use Reyes' image further—they could not be indifferent to the dishes which were being offered. On the contrary they were eager to try them. They were not primitive men but mature spirits for whom civilization was a vital necessity. At that moment, however, they found themselves in the midst of a primitive world which could not provide their needs. A rare example of genius among American caudillos, Bolívar showed clear judgment in saying, among other things, that "We are neither Europeans nor Indians, but an intermediate species between the aboriginal and the Spanish. Americans by birth, Europeans by right . . . so it is that our case is the most extraordinary and the most complicated."

The civilizing endeavors of Spain, meritorious as they may have been, were not adequate to overcome the difficulties of the American world. The problem lay, especially, in the need to populate the enormous expanse of the New Continent. And Spain at the time had neither a surplus of population which could emigrate nor a real intention of colonizing America. Her purpose was exploitation. Throughout our history the question has therefore defied solution. As late as the nineteenth century, the Argentinian Alberdi asserted that "in America, to civilize is to populate."

The isolation of Mexico, in effect, weakened the primal energy of the Spanish race. A handful of men scattered throughout an immense territory and separated, moreover, by a chaotic geography, were forced into a feeling of inferiority to the sea of nature surrounding them. Civilization slowly appeared on islands in the midst of that wilderness. In lonely stations of civilized life, the race was losing its adventurous dynamism, and passed from the tradition of action to the conventual life of the colonial era. Having achieved some degree of social, political, and economic stability, New Spain was nevertheless unable to reproduce integrally the life of the mother country. Men were no longer the same, for the Indian had altered their white visages with a trace of color. They lived in a different land, breathed a different atmosphere, contemplated a different landscape. In a word, they inhabited a new world. Here the old culture seemed dismembered and abstract. Historical destiny placed those men in the midst of two worlds which were only partially theirs. They were no longer Europeans, because they were living in America; nor were they Americans, because their inherent nature preserved their European sense of life. This initial psychological conflict has affected the particular events of our history.

Colonial Servitude
Justo Sierra wrote:

The measures taken by Spanish authority to subjugate or assimilate once and for all the cultural groups of America reach their peak of intensity in the eighteenth century. But since in that same epoch Spain ceases to be a first-ranking power— because she foolishly squanders her wealth and blood, because she ceases to be a great maritime power while continuing to be a great colonial power (an incongruity which was to result in the dissolution of her American empire), and because she never could be a real colonizer, given the scarcity of her population, there is a paralysis in the development of New Spain. Everything is consolidated, but the whole consolidation remains, so to speak, amortized in the routine and status quo. The seventeenth century is one of creation; the eighteenth century is one of preservation; the century following is one of fragmentation. Under these deceptive conditions social progress continues its slow march.[6]

From the beginning, colonial organization tended to depress the spirit of the new race. The conquerors were not workmen, but soldiers, who had to utilize the vanquished race in order to take advantage of their new possessions. Work in America did not, therefore, signify a benefit which could alleviate need but an opprobrium suffered for the benefit of the masters. Mexican will and initiative lacked opportunity for development. Wealth was not acquired by work but by the unjust privilege which permitted exploitation of the poor. Trade was the monopoly of the classic Spanish storekeeper, who came to America only to carry back a fortune to his native land. Mining and agriculture were sources of a wealth which also escaped to Europe. A few among the privileged classes were educated in schools and could later take up a profession. But the professions were practically reduced to two: the priesthood and the law. For the middle class the best means of earning a living was administrative work. Thus the majority of the population were reduced to inactivity, and became lazy and resigned to poverty. Out of this they had no hope of rising, other than God's favor in the form of a lottery prize. Since the wealth produced was withdrawn from Mexico, it is no surprise that the social economy was disastrously affected. This atmos-

[6] *México y su evolucion social*, I, 113.

phere was scarcely propitious to a strengthening of Mexican character. Having accentuated these vices of administration, Spain's decadence now reverberates injuriously in the contemporary Mexican's psychology. The monotonous and routine life of New Spain tended to perpetuate the inertia of will and to destroy every stimulus to novelty in the Mexican spirit. The Spanish government was very cautious to see that men or ideas that might disturb those stagnant waters did not reach the colony from other parts of the world. The monotonous rhythm has persisted in Mexico up to our time; it is still visible in village life, which moves on with a sluggishness similar to the immutability of Asiatic existence.

Indigenous "Egyptianism"[7]

Perhaps this inflexibility derives from the native spirit. We do not believe that the Indian's passivity is the result only of the enslavement which befell him at the time of the Conquest. Quite possibly he submitted to conquest because he was naturally inclined to passivity. Even before the Conquest natives were set against all forms of change and renovation. They stuck to their traditions and were routine and conservative by character. A will to the immutable was engraved on their style of culture.

In their art, for instance, a tendency to repeat the same forms is clearly noticeable. One deduces from this the existence of an academic kind of artistic production rather than a truly creative activity. Even today, popular indigenous art is the unvarying reproduction of one

[7] *egipticismo*, i.e., immutability.

model. Today's Indian is not an artist; he is an artisan who constructs his works by a skill learned in tradition.

The monumental artistic style of the pre-Cortesian Era reveals little fancy and is almost always dominated by a ritualistic formalism. In sculpture heavy masses abound; the resultant impression is of something unyielding and static. Instead of fusing the stone with a suggestion of movement, the artistic forms seem to increase its inorganic heaviness. Artistic expression of the Mexican plateau embodies the rigidity of death. It seems as though the hardness of stone had subdued the fluidity of life. By an inevitable association, contemplation of Mexican art brings to mind the Egyptian spirit. Worringer says:

Rigidity, inhuman, extra-human rigidity, is the mark of that culture. How could there have been room in it for the eternal flow of space? There is no doubt that rigidity can also acquire high value. But this depends on vitality, that is, on the vitality overcome by that rigidity. There is a demoniac rigidity, a rigidity in which a respectful tremor, man's richest endowment, reaches a sublime conquest and a sublime repose. But there is also another rigidity, sober and arid, based upon an internal antagonism and insensibility for the deepest vibrations of life. It seems to me that Egyptian rigidity is the equivalent of this last type. It does not set forth a static being as the vanquisher of a dynamic *becoming;* it is rather a being which precedes all becoming, or comes entirely after it.

If the Mexican Indian seems unassimilable to civilization it is not because he is inferior to it, but *different* from it. His "Egyptianism" makes him incompatible with a civilization whose law is to "become." As if by magic influence, native "Egyptianism" (immutability) seems to have touched all men and things in Mexico, men and things which accordingly resist the pull of the torrent of universal evolution. Novelty interests us only when it is superficial, like a fashion. For its age, Mexico has changed very little. Our changes are more apparent than real; they are but diverse masks that conceal a single spiritual character.

The Native and Civilization

The inhabitant of Mexico City frequently forgets the coexistence in his country of two diverse and scarcely related worlds. One is primitive and belongs to the Indian; the other is civilized and is the white man's domain. But the white man can perceive this dualism simply by examining in his own conscience the agitation and incompatibility between primitive and civilized motives, which are at times in dramatic conflict. Keyserling noticed this psychological dualism in South America and considered it a refining equilibrium which man possesses in spite of his primitive origin. There is no doubt that this strange phenomenon must be called a universal trait of Spanish-American character.

To be sure, the soul of the pure-blooded Indian does not share the dualism, but the Indian's presence creates the dualism in our civilization. Still here before us, the Indian is today more enigmatic than ever. A priori, a spirit similar to the white man's has been attributed to him: the theory being that its development has simply been retarded. The Indians seem to constitute a race of minors who must be treated as children. However, more attentive psychological observation will prove the falsity of this viewpoint. If the indigenous spirit does not differ substantially from that of the white man, why that disconcerting indifference and scorn? Why even the resistance to a civilization which is visibly superior to his own? Such an attitude cannot be interpreted as a sign of mental inferiority, for the numerous natives who live in the society of whites have demonstrated the same capacity as the latter for higher civilization. Pure-blooded Indians have excelled in the various professions, political positions, and branches of culture. Are not these facts emphatic proof that the Indian is fit to assimilate civilization? Yes, but they are also proof that the fitness does not show unless the individual is separated from the social group in which he was born. So long as he remains in the indigenous environment, the individual is subservient to a collective conscience which is steeped and consolidated in its traditions. He feels that all the strange elements of civilization are incompatible with his nature. We have here a characteristic reaction of native American cultures, and it is indispensable to our understanding of their spirit.

In primitive communities culture and life form an inseparable whole, so that every detail in the behavior of individuals—at work, at home, in public life, and even in personal appearance—is considered essential to the preservation of its unity. Such communities are therefore hostile to innovations, especially when they come from the outside. For the white man, a suit of clothes or an instrument is simply a useful object which he is ready to abandon at any moment, provided he is offered another suit or instrument that will serve him better. For the Indian, the useful properties of things and of the instruments which he manufactures exist in proportion to their mystic relationship with all being. Before the Conquest, Indians attributed the invention and foundation of everything beneficial to certain civilizing deities, for example, Ku-kulkan among the Mayas. In those times abandonment or substitution of one technical procedure or tradition for another signified sacrilege. Today's Indian has forgotten his history but the unconscious mechanism of his acts still operates in the same way.

The indigenous spirit was tolerant enough to allow the influence of similar races. This was the case with the Mayas in their relationship with the Aztecs. But the encounter of the indigenous spirit with European civilization in the sixteenth century brought about a complete change of attitude. It would seem that the Indians' resistance to civilization might be traced to popular resentment against a dominating race which mistreated and humiliated them; the Indian cannot be expected to have affection for the civilization that has caused his affliction. But this historical fact does not explain sufficiently well the difficulties entailed in civilizing him.

Even if the Conquest had been undertaken in a humanitarian way, and had the colonial domination been less rigid—in a word, even if the white race had not become odious to the native, the latter would still have resisted civilization. Peculiar psychological motives were involved.

In all primitive races there is some degree of uniformity in their interpretation of the white man's arrival. He is usually depicted as a great wizard whose presence occasions evil. In the myth of Quetzalcoatl the white man assumes divine proportions and the Aztecs had a presentiment that the advent of the white man would be a catastrophe for them. Primitive man is incapable of separating in his thought the virtues of an instrument or machine from the virtues of the being which has devised them. He attributes the efficiency of instruments and machines used by the white man to the relationship between the society in which the white man lives and some extraordinary mystic personality. The instruments and machines, therefore, are good for the white man, but not for the Indian. Only insofar as the individual associates himself with a group which enjoys the protection of certain divinities, are the instruments useful. Herein lies the primitive man's concept of the world. Manufactured objects are included in the mystic totality of civilization and society. If separated from that totality, the objects lose their qualities. This psychological mechanism explains the indigenous spirit's dread of novelty and its impermeability to modern culture. Only an external compulsion can cause the native to alter his customs or his techniques; and just as soon as the compulsion ceases, the Indian turns back to his old ways. It is disconcerting to note that when he is given a choice of two models—one, indigenous, crude, and inconvenient, and the other, foreign, refined, and more efficient, the Indian will invariably prefer the former. Like other modern things, machines and their effects are explained by magic principles whose secret only the white man possesses. Consequently, the native must choose his own deficient tools. In this negative reaction of the native to techniques superior to his own, one can see that behind every thought and act lies a religious sentiment which is the mainspring of his soul.

The Beginnings of Independent Life

Happily for the social evolution of Mexico, immutability is not the only force that has acted upon our collective life. Since the beginning of the nineteenth century the direction of our history has been in the hands of dynamic minorities well acquainted with modern ideas from Europe. Having won her independence, Mexico had no desire to continue living in antiquated patterns of existence. But the stigmata remaining from the Colonial Era diverted her effort and created progressively more confusing complications—to the extent that a way out was almost impossible to find. Certainly Mexicans lacked neither the intelligence nor the ability to improve their national life, but their will had grown numb during the Colonial Period of inertia. They had been unaware of this circumstance because they had not enjoyed free exercise of their will. But now, in the urgency of reorganizing their country, they recognized the defect. Though they sensed that their will was flagging, their weakness was not real; the defect was due in part to infrequent activity, and in part to a disproportion of the will to the magnitude of their plans. Mexicans wanted to make a *tabula rasa* of the past and begin a new life, as if they were just beginning to exist. But superior to man's will is a biological law which precludes any fundamental suppression of the past; the past inevitably affects present conduct. What Mexicans were attempting at that moment, not proudly but rashly, was to turn their backs on their own destiny. By *destiny* we mean precisely those forces which have inevitable effects on our lives. Though unaware of what they were doing, the men who declared our free nationality took on a superhuman task, and even the strongest of races would have felt unequal to an enterprise of such magnitude. We have emphasized the disproportion between real possibilities and the ideal which those men pursued, because it was the beginning of an experience which has been permanently harmful to the Mexican subconscious.

Unaccustomed to freedom of action, when confronted by their first difficulties they show a sense of inferiority. To interpret this judgment as an urge of ours to disdain the Mexican race would be most shortsighted. We do not mean to suggest that the inferiority is real. Quite obviously, we do not believe in the theory of inferior races, which seemed feasible while European culture was still considered an absolute value. From precisely this point of view, Hegel (in his *Lessons in the Philosophy of History*) attributes a positive inferiority to Americans. Mexicans themselves believed this in the past century and even formulated a self-denigratory thesis. But our idea must not be taken as just another self-denigration. On the contrary, we sincerely wish to show how that sentiment lacks an objective basis. Up to now biologists of our race have found no premise on which to infer that it has been affected by some organic or functional degeneration.

On the other hand, critical revision of European culture made on the basis of new philosophical viewpoints has greatly altered the position of absolute pre-eminence it held before World War I. Ideological currents which are anti-intellectualist because of the value they concede to irrational elements of life have permitted a more just appraisal of the "colored races" previously disdained. The biological question of intermarriage is still so much disputed that nothing can be concluded regarding its influence on the improvement or degeneration of races.

Reactions against a sentiment of inferiority—which in themselves prove the existence of that sentiment—include all those movements which tend to extoll the individual or collective personality. For example, Baron von Humboldt created the myth that in resources Mexico is the richest country in the world; but instead of becoming inspirational as a principle for practical action, the myth has been taken as an article of faith to flatter patriotic vanity and conceal real misery. The utopian idealism of free Mexicans, which aspires to implant here a political system including all the modern perfections without taking into account the real limitations of our circumstances, may also be considered a reaction to the sentiment of inferiority. The calamities of Mexican history in the nineteenth century are not due to an internal deficiency of race, but to the excessive ambition of governing minorities, who, obsessed with fantastic plans for national administration, overlooked the real problem of the Mexican people. Once independence was achieved the situation was this: a heterogeneous race geographically isolated by wide expanses of territory; a wretched and uncultured population, passive and indifferent like the Indian, accustomed to dissolute life; and a dynamic and educated minority, whose individualism was nevertheless aggravated by a sense of inferiority, antagonistic to all order and discipline. The most pressing problems, then, were economics and education. The political problem was secondary.

However, only the political problem was attacked, and with an idealism totally blind to the lessons of experience. The Mexican is idealistic because idealism exalts the idea he has of his own personality. Individualist that he is, he devotes his effort not to any specific project, but rather to an affirmation of himself as an individual. When reality opposes itself irremediably to the achievement of his projects, he does not renounce his purpose but unconsciously strives to attain a new fictional level of existence. Thus, albeit in an illusory way, the urge to assert his individuality is satisfied. With these ideas we conclude the theory of Mexican mimetism outlined at the beginning of this chapter.

II.
The Influence
of France
in the
Nineteenth
Century

*The Intellectuals of the
Independence Movement*

Having pointed out the harmful consequences of imitation, one might ask whether its constant practice has not ultimately benefited Mexican culture. By its very nature, imitation has always reproduced cultural superficialities by bringing together the external manifestations of spirit and culture. But does a person never comprehend the basic principles on which his culture rests? And conversely, may culture never penetrate to the depths of the Mexican soul? Undoubtedly both things have occurred. The prevailing personality of the past century was that of the mestizo. His favorite passion was politics. His standard of activity was candid imitation. The country he enthusiastically admired was France, which he considered the archetype of modern civilization. When something he wished to reproduce from French culture became an obsession, it developed as a substantial element of his spirit, as if because of a high emotional fever. Mexicans were attracted to France by the appeal of her political ideas, which served as a means of introduction to all French culture. Political passion was active in the assimilation of Spanish culture. What began as a sacrifice to foreign elements later became second nature. There is no doubt that the artificial components of our history are conditioned by something that is not artificial. France was not, in the nineteenth century, the most politically advanced country. England then occupied the vanguard. Why, then, did Mexicans choose France as a model? If the Mexican had not been psychologically predisposed to understand French culture, it would not have awakened his interest. And what affinities were there between Mexican and Frenchman? The revolutionary spirit of France offered the younger educated generation of Mexico the necessary principles with which to combat the past. Against political oppression, liberalism; against the monarchic state, a democratic republic; against clericalism, Jacobinism and secularism. The most intelligent and active group in Mexican society proposed to use French ideology as a weapon for the destruction of old institutions.

During the reign of Charles III in Spain, the American colonies enjoyed some benefits. Overseas trade was facilitated, a circumstance which also facilitated the importation of some new ideas. Charles III encouraged elementary and higher education in Mexico. It was then that public and private schools began to flourish; among the latter was San Francisco de Sales in San Miguel el Grande, which, under the direction of the distinguished philosopher, Dr. Gamarra, had

a curriculum equal to those developed in Europe in the institutions of greatest fame, and this institution was the first in Mexico to offer a complete course in modern philosophy, relegating to oblivion the Aristotelian school and replacing it with the Cartesian. As ideological precursor of our emancipation, this institution strongly urged the youth of the period to devote themselves to the study of mathematics as a basis for scientific education; and with the publication of his notable work, *Errors of Human Understanding*, Gamara combatted the social vices and problems of that era, setting the course to be followed later in the *Pensador Mexicano* and the *Pavo de Rosario* (periodicals). In this work of preparation and social transformation the creole Jesuits must not be forgotten: Clavijero, Abad, Alegre, Guevara, and so many others who in the schools of the Society disseminated new ideas which anticipated the organization of the Independence movement.[1]

So it was that intellectuals of New Spain, who were almost exclusively clergymen, laid the groundwork for this great event in our history.

The Royal and Pontifical Seminary of Mexico was a center of insurrection. One seminarist, Pastor Morales, was tried by the Inquisition for his devotion to the French

[1] Nicolás Rangel, *Preliminar a los precursores ideológicos de la Independencia, 1789–1794*, México, 1929, Publicaciones del Archivo General de la Nación.

Encyclopedists. Certain passages from the extract of the trial—quoted in the work by Nicolás Rangel just mentioned, and transcribed herewith—are of curious interest:

A certain individual, native of this America and about twenty-five years of age, a student in the schools of this capital, has studied modern philosophy and sacred theology, in which he has been graded superior because of his exceptional talent; he is devoted to the Latin poets, particularly Terence, Horace, and Metastasius, and to modern French books in whose reading he took special delight. His boredom with scholastic theological subjects has also induced him to think and speak with freedom and abandon. He is reputed to be imaginative, erudite and cultured, and he is quiet yet gracefully eloquent at the proper moment. He has said and done the following:

1) This individual has declared himself in many conversations to be a Francophile, principally on points of liberty and independence, on defending and approving the republican system, and on the execution of Louis XVI, king of France; he has also said, speaking of popular sovereignty, that when the king fails to fulfill his duties, his government is ineffective in bringing happiness to the people, in which case he defends the authority of peoples . . .

He is accused, furthermore, of reading prohibited books and of professing the ideology of new liberal philosophers like Voltaire, Rosseau, and D'Alembert. There were innumerable cases similar to this one, which suffices to show in a typical way the role of sentiment in the "Gallicization" of our spirit.

The quick assimilation of French ideas in Mexico was also due to a common Latin background and the resulting spiritual affinity between our country and France. Mexico had been Latinized by the double influence of the Catholic Church and Roman law. The courses of study available in schools and universities during the Colonial period were based on three fundamental disciplines: philosophy, theology, and law. Of the professions there were but two to choose from: priesthood and the law. Ever since that time the most authoritative figure in the eyes of the people has been—after the priest—the lawyer, or *licenciado*, as he is called in Mexico. Law then acquires the prestige of a sacrosanct fetish; but since life in all its variety does not lend itself to restriction within rigid formulas, legality is constantly violated, and the resultant impression is one of incongruous behavior. This trait is no exclusive feature of Mexican life; it is general throughout Latin America, a fact which we can appreciate on reading the following passage from a well-known French writer, André Siegfried:

Never have I heard so much talk about Constitutions as in those countries where the constitution is violated every day. Eminent jurists gravely and conscientiously discuss the significance of texts that are mocked by politicians, and in answer to ironical smiles, the magistrates count out on their fingers those articles which guarantee the law. The law has majesty in words only.[2]

Our race has acquired all the qualities and defects of the Latin spirit. F. García Calderón—"the Tocqueville of Latin America," as André Siegfried has called him— asks in one of the most interesting chapters of his book whether we Americans are of the Latin race, and answers affirmatively.

The qualities and defects of the classical spirit are revealed in American life: its tenacious idealism which underrates all attainment of the useful; its ideas of humanity, equality, and

[2] *Amérique Latine*, p. 100.

universality, notwithstanding a variety of races; its formalist cult; Latin vivacity and instability; faith in pure ideas and political dogmas. In these lands across the sea, all this is found, as well as a brilliant and superficial intelligence, Jacobinism, and oratorical facility. Enthusiasm and optimism are also Spanish American qualities.

These republics are not sheltered from any of the common weaknesses of Latin races. The State is omnipotent, the liberal-arts professions are overdeveloped, the power of bureaucracy is disturbing. The character of their citizens is weak, inferior to their imagination and their intelligence: concepts of union and spiritual solidarity struggle against an innate lack of discipline in the race. Dominated by exterior demands and by the tumult of politics, these men lack interior life; neither great mystics nor great poets are found among them. Against common realities they raise their exasperated individualism.

French Culture

French culture represents, in modern times, the survival of the classical spirit. It derives from the finest ingredients of Greek, Roman, and Italian Renaissance cultures which as a tradition have endured until our own day. Acquaintance with the essential features of that classical culture will help us understand the attraction which France has held for Hispanic America.[3] France acquired her Latin character in the period extending from Caesar to Charlemagne. It was then that a Romanization of the Gallic spirit took place. When the Franks, under Clovis, invaded Gaul, they had nothing that measured up to Gallo-Roman culture. Consequently,

[3] We are indebted in this exposition to the German writer Ernst Robert Curtius, who has produced a monumental study on the French mind and civilization, *Essai sur la France*, (Grasset, 1932), and also to Salvador de Madariaga, *Franceses, ingleses, españoles* (Espasa-Calpe).

they adapted themselves to it and assimilated it. "If Caesar's conquest resulted in the Romanization of Gaul, Clovis' conquest incited a Romanization of the Franks."[4] In later history French culture follows the same pattern of assimilation of the Latin spirit.

French cultural traits reach their definitive form in the "grand century" which was dominated by the dazzling figure of Louis XIV. French classicism was not an imitative style; it dates from that same era. Everywhere—in art, architecture, poetry, and gardening—we see the same aesthetic inclination to dominate the overflowings of fantasy by rationalistic techniques. Thus the characteristic traits of French culture were born. According to Curtius, the universal works were created with an eye to national realities. But it was the Latin tradition that engraved on that culture its rationalism, formality, logical order, and universality.

The cultural treasure of France is not composed of unique visions of the world that surpass the level of common understanding. France, says Curtius, is a *terre du milieu*; in like manner, its literature is a *littérature du milieu*. "What distinguishes it is neither the sustained height of inspiration, nor the profundity of its cosmic sentiment. It is the harmonious equilibrium which it has succeeded in establishing in the passive regions of its spirit." French culture has a common scale of values that every Frenchman can consider his own, and in which every Frenchman can participate. However, the Frenchman does not conceive of his culture as *French*, but as a universal culture created for all men. The penetration of this notion of French culture in Mexico suggests the in-

4 Curtius, *op. cit.*

herent attraction of propaganda, which always found in our country an appropriate atmosphere.

Since French culture is quite normal, in that it has developed as a continuation of Renaissance humanism, it possesses—of all modern cultures—the greatest human substance; and its literature, for example, is a "continuous discourse on man." For a Frenchman, the word *culture* does not signify spiritual works alone, but also a certain order of all life within rational norms. Culture is also discernible in the commonest acts of man, such as eating, conversing, making love.

From the "humanistic" aspect of French culture comes a certain "utilitarian" value which is its possible application to the practical service of man. That "utility" is one of the virtues which has made French culture attractive for Hispanic Americans. It has been truthfully said that in Hispanic America the only ideas that take root are those which may be politically or socially useful. In this sense we should recall the example of positivism, which found acceptance in Mexico by virtue of its political utility; it was a theory favorable to liberalism and Jacobinism. Some of the Mexicans' "elective affinities" can be explained if we compare the preceding concept with the following concept from Curtius on philosophy:

The greater part of the French nation did not take an interest in philosophy until the day philosophy abandoned the field of pure abstraction and presented itself as an aggregate of sciences—whose object was human life and the world, as an instrument working for political emancipation, and as a harbinger of new social forms: in a word, as an ally of science (p. 160).

Count Keyserling has published a chaotic volume

(*South American Meditations*) in which we find very good observations on Hispanic-American character and life obscured by a cloud of metaphysical fantasies. A valuable excerpt, free of the scoria with which the author so gratuitously padded his book, is a brief article entitled "South American Perspectives," which was published in the Argentine review, *Sur*, before *South American Meditations* came out. The term *South American* should be taken in the European sense, which includes all countries to the south of the United States. Keyserling himself, in his *Meditations*, alludes frequently to Mexico; so we are authorized to consider the German philosopher's ideas as pertinent to our country also. Keyserling observes that what characterizes the psychological atmosphere of South America is "a synthesis of the primordial and the refined." The notion is important to us now only insofar as it can be related to our theme of French culture. It makes us understand the apparently incomprehensible: that countries which have only recently accepted civilization are receptive to a style of delicate tones that for its final development has required a previous and extensive historical evolution in France. But it is also true that the Hispanic American, particularly the inhabitant of the tablelands, naturally possesses the refinement that Keyserling refers to and has therefore been able to grasp the sense of nuances peculiar to French artistic form. And there exists in the more modern styles of the latter, a sensuality—possibly of Mediterranean origin—which easily adapts itself to our own tropical sensuality. Despite the fact that as the nineteenth century progresses the Anglo-Saxon manner has a certain impact on Hispanic American life, one can affirm that the Mexicans' efforts to obtain a scientific, artistic, philosophical, and literary culture are guided by the magic symbol of France. This spiritual influence reaches its height in the epoch of Porfirio Díaz, when the cultured classes dressed according to the Parisian vogue and imitated its good and bad customs. The "scientists,"[5] and the wealthy who were not scientific, adorned their houses with mansard roofs, even though it never snows in Mexico. To be a cultured person knowledge of the French language was a *sine-qua-non* condition. The Mexican atmosphere was saturated with French ideas, to the point where domestic realities were ignored. This was to provoke a strong reaction, in which the Mexican openly refused to conform to a predominating European culture.

[5] "Scientists," or more precisely, "scientific ones" (*científicos*) was the label given those leaders of the Porfirio Díaz era who identified themselves with positivistic, Darwinian, and Spencerian doctrines. (Translator's note)

III.
Psychoanalysis
of the
Mexican

ow big a dose of truth can man endure?" Nietzsche's question comes to mind as we complete our notes for the present chapter, and we are moved to warn the reader about its content, which is a blunt but dispassionate exposition of what we believe constitutes Mexican psychology. To deduce from this an adverse judgment of the Mexican would be to abuse our thesis. We do not make him responsible for his present character, which is the effect of a historical fate superior to his will. It is not very flattering to be identified with a character such as the one about to be described. But it is a relief to know that this character which conceals our authentic being can be changed—just like a suit of clothes —because it has been borrowed. In this instance our problem is not one of self-denigration, nor of an obsession to speak about unpleasant things with the sole purpose of "shocking the bourgeois."

We are among the first to admit that certain regions of the human soul should remain a mystery, when nothing can be gained by exposing them to the light of day. But it seems harmful for the Mexican to close his eyes to his own character when it works against his destiny; he cannot change his character without first becoming specifically aware of it. In such cases truth is more salutary than a life of self-deception. Be it noted that we are not restricting ourselves in this essay to a description of the most salient features of Mexican character, but are rather probing deep so as to discover its hidden causes. Thus we may find a way of rejuvenating our soul.

The purpose of this study is not to criticize Mexicans with malign intent. It is every Mexican's right, we believe, to analyze his soul and to publish freely his observations, so long as he is convinced that these, disagreeable or not, will be advantageous to others, and so long as he shows how within himself mysterious forces exist which, if not noticed in time, are likely to frustrate his vitality. Men unaccustomed to criticism believe that everything that is not praise works against them, when actually to praise such men is the surest way of working against them and of doing them harm.

Others have spoken of the sense of inferiority in our race; but no one, so far as I know, has systematically utilized the concept to explain our character. In this essay a methodical application of Adler's psychological theories to the Mexican is attempted for the first time. One must presuppose the existence of an inferiority complex in all thoses people who show an excessive concern with affirming their personality, who take vital interest in all things and situations that signify power, and who demonstrate an immoderate eagerness to excel, to be first in everything. Adler states that the inferiority complex appears in a child as soon as he recognizes the insignificance of his own strength compared to the strength of his parents. Mexico at first found itself in the same relationship to the civilized world as that of the child to his parents. It entered Western history at a time when a mature civilization already prevailed, something which an infantile spirit can only half understand. This disadvantageous circumstance induced the sense of inferiority that was aggravated by conquest, racial commingling, and even the disproportionate magnitude of nature. But this sense is not actually perceptible in Mexican behavior until the time of the Independence movement in the first third of the past century.[1]

It seems unnecessary to base this conclusion on an accumulation of documents. If the reader is sincerely interested in the problem and accepts these ideas in good

[1] "As for young nations," says Keyserling, "they do not have a concentrated and critical spirit. They are spiritually passive, like all young beings; they are very easily influenced and accept bad criticism because of a weakness which is both physiological and moral; they are constantly perturbed by a sense of inferiority." (*L'Avenir de l'esprit européen*, Edition de l'Institut de Cooperation Intelectuelle, 1934, p. 28.)

faith, he will find confirmation in his own observations. Before going into case histories from Mexican life, we have thought it desirable to state how a person's mind *generally* functions, what its habitual reactions are, and what inducements it obeys.

There is no reason why the reader should be offended by these pages, in which the affirmation is not that the Mexican *is* inferior, but rather that he *feels* inferior. This is quite different. If, in certain individual cases, the sense of inferiority discloses real organic or psychic deficiencies, for the majority of Mexicans it constitutes a collective illusion which results from measuring man against the very high scales of values corresponding to highly developed countries. We ask the reader, therefore, to examine our ideas with absolute equanimity. If, despite these explanations, the reader is hurt, we are sincerely sorry, but we will prove that there exists in our countries of America, as Keyserling puts it, "a propensity to being offended"; thus, an indignant reaction would be the most resounding proof of our thesis.

The Pelado[2]

To discover the motivating force of the Mexican soul it was first necessary to review a few of its great collective movements. Plato maintained that the state is an enlarged image of the individual. We shall demonstrate in like manner that the Mexican behaves in his private world the same as he does in public life.

[2] *Pelado*. This past participle and adjective has in Spanish the several literal meanings of "plucked," "bare," "peeled," "treeless," "husked," "penniless." As the designation of a universally familiar social type in Mexico, it defies translation into English. However, the pages immediately following offer a precise characterization of the *pelado*. (Translator's note)

The Mexican psyche is the result of reactions that strive to conceal an inferiority complex. In the first chapter of this book we explained that such concealment is achieved by falsifying the image of the external world, exalting in that way the Mexican's consciousness of his own worth. In his own country he imitates modes of European civilization in order to feel that he is equal to the European, and in order to establish in his cities a privileged group which considers itself superior to all those Mexicans who live beyond the borders of civilization. But this fictional process does not end with exterior things, nor is it enough to restore the psychological equilibrium that the inferiority complex has destroyed. The same process is also applicable to the individual and falsifies his own idea of himself. Psychoanalysis of the individual Mexican is the topic which we shall now undertake.

To understand the mechanism of the Mexican mind, we shall examine it in context that reveals how all its movements are exacerbated; thus the sense of that mind's development will be clearly perceptible. The best model for study is the Mexican *pelado*, for he constitutes the most elemental and clearly defined expression of national character. We shall say nothing of his picturesque aspect, which has been represented to the point of tedium in the popular theater, in the novel, and in painting. Our only interest here is his inner self and the elemental forces that determine his character. His name (*pelado*) defines him accurately. He is the kind of person who continually lays bare his soul, so that its most intimate confines are visible. He brazenly flaunts certain elemental impulses which other men try to dissimulate. The *pelado* belongs to a most vile category of social fauna; he is a form of human rubbish from the great city. He is less than a proletarian in the economic hierarchy, and a primitive man in the intellectual one. Life from every quarter has been hostile to him and his reaction has been black resentment. He is an explosive being with whom relationship is dangerous, for the slightest friction causes him to blow up. His explosions are verbal and reiterate his theme of self-affirmation in crude and suggestive language. He has created a dialectic of his own, a diction which abounds in ordinary words, but he gives these words a new meaning. He is an animal whose ferocious pantomimes are designed to terrify others, making them believe that he is stronger than they and more determined. Such reactions are illusory retaliations against his real position in life, which is a nullity. This disagreeable truth strives to force its way up to the surface of his conscience, but it is impeded by another force which from within the subconscious consistently reduces his sense of personal integrity. Any exterior circumstance that might aggravate his sense of inferiority will provoke a violent reprisal, the aim of which is to subdue his depression. The result is a constant irritability that incites him to fight with others on the most insignificant pretext. But his bellicose spirit does not derive from a sentiment of hostility toward all humanity. The *pelado* seeks out quarrels as a stimulus, to renew the vigor of his downtrodden ego. He needs a support for recovering faith in himself, but since his support is devoid of all real value, he has to replace it with a fictitious one. He is like a shipwreck victim who, after flailing about in a sea of nothingness, suddenly discovers his driftwood of salvation: virility. The *pelado's* terminology abounds in sexual allusions which reveal his phallic obsession; the sexual organ becomes symbolic of masculine force. In verbal combat he attributes to his adversary an imaginary femininity, reserving for himself the masculine role. By this strategem he pretends to assert his superiority over his opponent.

We should like to illustrate these theories, but unfortunately, the *pelado's* language is so crudely realistic that it is not possible to transcribe many of his most characteristic phrases. Nevertheless, certain typical expressions cannot be ignored. The reader should not take offense at our citation of words which in Mexico are used only in intimate conversations. Beyond their vulgarity and grossness the psychologist can discern a different and more noble sense. And it would be unpardonable to disregard such valuable material for study under the pretext of acceding to a dubiously conceived notion of decency in language. It would be comparable to a chemist's refusing to analyze all substances that smell bad.

The most destitute of Mexican *pelados* consoles himself by shouting at everyone that "he's got balls" (*muchos huevos*)[3] with reference to the testicles. It is important to note that he attributes to the reproductive organ not only one kind of potency, the sexual, but every kind of human power. In the *pelado* a man who triumphs in any activity, anywhere, owes his success to his "balls." Another of his favorite expressions, "I am your father" (*Yo soy tu padre*), intends to assert his predominance unequivocally. In our patriarchal societies the father is for all men the symbol of power. It must also be remarked that the *pelado's* phallic obsession is not comparable to

[3] *muchos huevos*, literally, "many eggs."

phallic cults and their underlying notions of fecundity and eternal life. The phallus suggests to the *pelado* the idea of power. From this he has derived a very impoverished concept of man. Since he is, in effect, a being without substance, he tries to fill his void with the only suggestive force accessible to him: that of the male animal. He turns this popular concept of man into a dismal view of all Mexicans. When a Mexican compares his own nullity to the character of a civilized foreigner, he consoles himself in the following way: "A European has science, art, technical knowledge, and so forth; we have none of that here, but . . . we are very manly." Manly in the zoological sense of the term, that is, in the sense of the male enjoying complete animal potency. The Mexican is fond of boasting and believes that he demonstrates this potency in courage. If only he knew that such courage is a smoke screen! Appearances must not, therefore, deceive us. The *pelado* is neither a strong nor a brave man. The appearance he shows us is false. It is a camouflage by which he misleads himself and all those who come into contact with him. One can infer that the more show he makes of courage and force, the greater is the weakness that he is trying to hide. However much the *pelado* deceives himself by this illusion, he can never be certain of his power, so long as his weakness is present and threatens to betray him. He lives in distrust of himself and in continuous fear of being discovered. So it is that his perception becomes abnormal; he imagines that the next man he encounters will be his enemy; he mistrusts all who approach him.

After this brief description of the Mexican *pelado*, an

outline of his mental structure and operation seems advisable for an eventual understanding of the Mexican's psychology in general.

   I. The *pelado* has two personalities: one real, the other, fictitious.

   II. His real personality is obscured by his fictitious one, or the one that first appears to himself and others.

   III. His fictitious personality is diametrically opposed to his real one, for the object of the first is to raise the psychic level depressed by the second.

   IV. Since this individual lacks real human value and is powerless to acquire it, he utilizes a ruse to conceal his sentiments of inferiority.

   V. The fictitious personality's lack of real foundation creates a sense of self-distrust.

   VI. Self-distrust produces abnormality in the psychic functioning, especially in the perception of reality.

   VII. This abnormal perception amounts to an unjustified distrust of others, in addition to a hypersensitivity in in his contact with other men.

   VIII. Since our subject lives in falsehood, his position is always unstable and obliges him to keep constant vigil over his ego, while consequently neglecting reality.

His lack of attention to reality and his correlative preoccupation with himself lend support to our classification of the *pelado* among the "introverts."

One might think that the *pelado's* inferiority complex is not due to the fact that he is Mexican, but rather to his proletarian status. Indeed, this status could be the logical result of the complex, but there are convincing reasons for assuming that it is not the only decisive factor in the *pelado's* personality. We also notice that he associates his concept of virility with that of nationality, creating thereby the illusion that personal valor is the Mexican's particular characteristic. To see how nationality in itself creates a feeling of inferiority, one need only note the susceptibility of the *pelado's* patriotic sentiments and his pompous expression of words and exclamations. The frequency of individual and collective patriotic manifestations is symbolic of the Mexican's insecurity about the value of his nationality. Decisive proof of this affirmation is found in the fact that the same sentiment exists in cultivated and intelligent Mexicans of the bourgeoisie.

The Mexican of the City

We turn now to the city dweller. His psychology is clearly different from that of the rural inhabitant, not only because of the kind of life the latter leads, but because the *campesino* in Mexico is almost always of the indigenous race. Even though the Indian constitutes a large proportion of the Mexican population, his role is a passive one in the present life of his country. The active group is that of the mestizos and whites who live in the city. One supposes, of course, that the Indian has influenced the soul of the other Mexican group, because he has mixed his blood with theirs. But his social and spiritual influence is today reduced to the simple fact of his presence. He is like a chorus who silently witnesses the drama of Mexican life. However, the restricted nature of his intervention does not mean that it is insignificant. The Indian is like those substances identified as "catalytic," the mere presence of which provokes chemical reactions. Nothing Mexican is immune to this influence, because the indigenous mass is like a dense atmosphere that envelops everything in the nation. We therefore might think of the Indian as the Mexican's human "hinterland." But the Indian is not at this moment the object of our investigation.

The most striking aspect of Mexican character, at first sight, is distrust. This attitude underlies all contact with men and things. It is present whether or not there is motivation for it. It is not a question of distrust on principle, because generally speaking the Mexican lacks principles. It is rather a matter of irrational distrust that emanates from the depths of his being. It is almost his primordial sense of life. Whether or not circumstances justify it, there is nothing in the universe which the Mexican does not see and evaluate through his distrust. It is like an a priori form of his oversensitivity. The Mexican does not distrust any man or woman in particular; he distrusts all men and all women. His distrust is not limited to the human race; it embraces all that exists and happens. If he is a businessman he doesn't believe in business; if he is a professional he doesn't believe in his profession; if he is a politician he doesn't believe in politics. It is the Mexican's view that ideas make no sense and he scornfully calls them "theories." He judges the knowledge of scientific principles as useless. He seems very confident of his practical insight, but as a man of action he is awkward and ultimately gives little credit to the efficacy of facts. He has no religion and professes no social or political creed. He is the least "idealistic" person imaginable. He unreasonably negates everything, because he is negation personified.

What then does the Mexican live for? He would perhaps reply that it is not necessary to have ideas and beliefs in order to live—provided that one does not think. And indeed, this is the situation. In its totality, Mexican life gives the impression of being an unreflecting activity, entirely without plan. In Mexico each man concerns himself only with immediate issues. He works for today and tomorrow but never for later on. The future is a preoccupation which he has banished from his conscience. He is incapable of adventure in projects that offer only remote results. He has therefore suppressed from his life one of its most important dimensions—the future. Such are the effects of Mexican distrust.

In a life limited to the present, only instinct can function. Intelligent reflection can intervene only in those pauses when one is able to suspend one's activity. It is impossible to think and act simultaneously. Thought presupposes that we are capable of expectation, and one who expects is receptive to the future. Obviously, a life without future can have no norms. Mexican life is accordingly at the mercy of the four winds; instead of sailing, it drifts. Men say that they live as God wills. With neither discipline nor organization, Mexican society not unnaturally finds itself in a chaos in which individual beings move unpredictably like dispersed atoms.

An immediate symptom of this chaotic world is its reliance on distrust which it instills in an almost objective way. When a man feels lost in a realm of instability, where he is uncertain even of the ground he walks on, his distrust increases and makes him hasten to wrest from the present moment its fullest value. Thus the horizon of his life shrinks and his moral sense dwindles to the extent that society, notwithstanding its compatibility with civilization, is like a primitive horde in which men quarrel like hungry beasts.

A trait intimately connected with distrust is susceptibility. The distrustful type is fearful of everything and lives vigilantly, on the defensive. He is suspicious of all gestures, movements, and words. He interprets everything as an offense. In this attitude the Mexican goes to unbelievable extremes. His perception has become clearly abnormal. Because of his extreme touchiness the Mexican quarrels constantly; he no longer awaits attack but steps forward in order to offend. These pathological reactions often lead him to excesses, even to the point of committing needless crimes.

The psychic anomalies just described undoubtedly arise from an insecurity of the self which the Mexican unconsciously projects, converting it into distrust of men and the world. These psychic transformations are instinctive tricks devised to protect the ego from itself. The initial phase of the series is an inferiority complex experienced as a distrust of self, which the individual objectifies in the form of distrust toward strangers. Thus he frees himself from the unpleasantness associated with that complex.

When the human psyche strives to rid itself of a disagreeable feeling, it invariably resorts to illusory processes like the one just described. But in this particular case such processes are unsatisfactory, because the veil covering the unwelcome affliction does not actually suppress it; it only brings about a change in its motivation. The Mexican is continually in a mood that betrays his inner malaise, his incompatibility with himself. He is sensitive and nervous, almost always in a bad humor, and often irate and violent.

The strength which the Mexican attributes to himself, relying on his impulsiveness, is unconvincing. Of course, real energy implies intelligent control of one's impulses, and, at times, suppression of them. The Mexican is passionate, aggressive, and warlike out of weakness; that is to say, he lacks the will to control his actions. On the other hand, the energy evolving from these acts surpasses his vitality, which, more often than not, is weak. How then, is the violence of his acts to be explained? Only by considering it as the result of a super-excitation that has caused his psychic disequilibrium.

Knowledge of the psychology of the Mexican would be incomplete without a comparison of his idea of himself with what he really is. We have just spoken of the strength that the Mexican attributes to himself; we consequently assume that he has a favorable idea of his personality. We suspect, furthermore, that some readers of this essay will react against our affirmations, seeking arguments to reject them. The fact is that here we have ventured to uncover certain truths which every Mexican strives to conceal; for he superimposes on these truths an image of himself that does not represent what he is, but what he would like to be. What is the strongest and most intimate desire of the Mexican? He would like to become one who, by dint of his valor and strength, lords it over others. He is artificially exalted by the suggestion of this image, and persuaded to work in harmony with it until such time as he actually believes in the reality of the phantom which he has fashioned out of himself.

The Middle-Class Mexican

In the final part of the present chapter we shall be concerned with the most intelligent and cultivated of the Mexicans, the greater part of whom belong to the middle class of the nation. The several qualities masking his character are a reaction against the sentiment of inferiority which, not having derived from an economic, intellectual, or social inferiority, originate in the mere circumstance of being Mexican. The middle-class Mexican does not differ essentially from the proletarian Mexican, except that for the latter the sense of inferiority is aggravated by a coincidence of two factors: nationality and social position. There seems to be a contrast between the rude and violent manner ever present in the proletarian city dweller and a certain gentility in the bourgeois, who expresses himself with frequently exaggerated courtesy. But any Mexican of the cultivated classes is susceptible, when a moment of anger causes him to lose his self-control, to the tone and language of the ill-bred. "You're acting like a *pelado!*" is a reproach commonly directed to such an irate person. The middle-class Mexican has the same patriotic oversensitivity as the man in the street and the same prejudices with regard to national character.

The main psychic disparity between upper-class Mexicans and those of the lower classes is due to a complete dissimulation by the former of their sense of inferiority; the tie between their manifest attitudes and their subconscious motivations is so indirect and subtle as to defy discovery. On the other hand, the *pelado* flaunts with impudent frankness his psychological idiosyncrasies, and the connection in his soul between the conscious and the unconscious is quite simple. We have already seen that it grows out of an incompatibility.

We can now appropriately point out what constitutes the feelings of inner weakness, and how they irritate the psyche and provoke the reactions already described. The conscience cannot tolerate these feelings, because of the unpleasantness and depression they create; and precisely because of the need to conceal them in the unconscious, they show up in the form of vague sensations of distress, the motive for which is inaccessible and undefinable to the individual. When these sentiments reach the level of consciousness they assume varied forms. Some of these are debility, self-denigration, and feelings of incompetence and of vital deficiency. The recognition which the person now gives to his inferiority transforms itself into self-distrust.

The middle-class Mexican possesses more intellectual gifts and resources than does the proletarian and can easily exercise the sham designed to conceal his inferiority complex. This means that the fictitious *ego* invented by each person is such an impressive achievement and has such verisimilitude, that it is almost indistinguishable from the true *ego*.

Definition of these elements that help the Mexican achieve his fiction is obviously necessary. In short, what reactions does his inferiority complex stir up? In its simplest form, the operation amounts to superimposing on one's real being the image of what one would like to be, and to interpreting this image as a reality. At times one's desire is limited to an avoidance of scorn or humiliation; but then, on an ascending scale, we would find this desire to be equally as important as others; next, to predominate over others; and finally, to have absolute authority.

Formation of a self-image in harmony with a desire for superiority necessitates constant self-concern and attention. Thus, every Mexican becomes an introvert, and at the same time he loses interest in his real self. He thinks of men and things as mirrors, recognizing only those which allow him to see the image that he wants reflected. It is essential that other men believe in this image also, so that his own faith in it may be strengthened. Thus he can achieve his work of fantasy with society's complicity. We do not suggest that this phenomenon is exclusively Mexican. No normal man, whatever his nationality, could live without similar fictions. But one thing is to accept pragmatically the influence of a fiction—knowing what it is; quite another is to experience it without becoming aware of its falsity. In the first instance, the ideals or archetypes sought after encourage one to surmount the hindrances and complexities of human life; while in the second instance, it is less a matter of living than cheating life. No moral characterization could be appropriately applied to this attitude, which does not derive from a conscious and deliberate plan. Recent psychological discoveries demonstrate that blindness is not the cause for an unknowing person's lack of logical sense, even if this sense be different from the rational. The Mexican is unaware of the fact that he is living a lie, because subconscious forces have impelled him to it. Perhaps, were he to become aware of the deception, he would cease living as he does.

Since self-deception consists of believing that one is already what one would like to be, the Mexican puts off all attempts at effective betterment so long as he is satisfied with his own image of himself. He is, then, a man who moves through the years without experiencing any change. With the transformation of the civilized world, emerge new forms of life, art, and thought which the Mexican strives to imitate, his ultimate purpose being to achieve a feeling of equality with European man. But the Mexican of today is substantially the same as the Mexican of one hundred years ago, and his life proceeds within the apparently modernized city as does that of the Indian in the country: that is, in an Egyptian immutability.

We can imagine the Mexican as a man who flees from himself to take refuge in a fictitious world. But his psychological drama does not thereby disappear. In the depths of his soul, scarcely accessible to his own contemplation, palpitates the uncertainty of his position. And, in obscure recognition of the inconsistency of his personality—likely to vanish at the slightest breath, he protects himself, like a porcupine, with a coating of quills. No one can touch him without being hurt. He is extraordinarily sensitive to criticism, and he holds it at bay, ever ready to thrust abusive language at his fellow man. For this same reason, self-criticism remains paralyzed. He needs to convince himself that others are inferior. He therefore admits no superiority and is ignorant of the meaning of veneration, respect, and discipline. He is ingenious in detracting from others to the point of annihilating them.

He practices slander with the cruelty of a cannibal. The ego cult is as bloodthirsty as the ancient Aztec ritual; it feeds on human victims. Each individual lives closed within himself, like an oyster within its shell, in a fixed gesture of distrust toward others, exuding malignity, so that no one will come close to him. He is indifferent to collective interests and his action is always individualistic by nature.

We conclude these notes on Mexican psychology by asking if it will perhaps be impossible to rid the Mexican of the phantom dwelling within him. It certainly would seem possible only if everyone were to practice the Socratic precept of "know thyself." We know today that the natural faculties of man are inadequate for acquiring self-knowledge; he must first equip himself with the intellectual tools devised by psychoanalysis. When, thus prepared, man discovers what he is, a solution to the remaining problems will follow automatically. Phantoms are nocturnal beings that vanish. They simply have to be exposed to the light of day.

IV.
Creole
Culture

Thee has been a persistent trend in
Mexican psychology to fabricate new destinies for all
levels of national life. While it is true that our notion of
Europeanism has usually deceived us, the ideal of gen-
erating a pure Mexicanism has been equally false. The
Mexican never takes into account the reality of his life,
that is, those limitations which history, race, and biological conditions impose on his future. The Mexican plans

his life as if he were free to choose any course of action that appealed to his imagination as interesting or valuable. He is unaware that the horizon of possibilities is extremely limited for every man and every people. Historical heredity, ethnic mental traits, and environmental peculiarities determine the evolution of life with a rigidity that individual wills can never alter. We call this fatalistic phenomenon "destiny."

The Mexican is a man who for years has devoted himself systematically to combatting his destiny. His attitude has led him to sow cultural seeds that can thrive only in a European climate, and that here on his own land have grown up weak and nearly lifeless—like greenhouse specimens. He is convinced, at last, of his failure; but misunderstanding its causes, he blames failure on failure itself, that is, on an imaginary fracture in European culture, and not—as he should—on a hidden flaw in his own psychology. In changing his plans he has therefore changed his outward objective, but the psychological mechanism remains the same: it is a strategem. He now proposes to invent a culture, a Mexican way of life, a utopia more extreme than the Europeanized one, because he now thinks he can create something from nothing. Or possibly the pretense is even a reconstruction of the entire process of world culture, beginning with the neolithic era. The most recent displays of nationalism make us fear that the Mexican, in the intimacy of his psychological world, has cheated himself, that he has concealed his true nature—of which he is ignorant—by the superimposition of a false image. The essential virtue for the Mexican of today is sincerity. Without it he cannot remove the mask with which he disguises his authentic being from himself.

Europeanism in Mexico has turned out to be a greenhouse culture, not because it is essentially foreign to us, but rather because of the false relationship to European circumstances in which we have placed ourselves. We must recognize the fact that our cultural perspectives are European by definition. Culture is not a matter of choice, like the brand of a hat. We have European blood, our language is European, our customs and morality are European, and the sum of our vices and virtues is a legacy of the Spanish race. All these things shape our destiny and inexorably mark out the route we are to follow. The main thing lacking is the wisdom necessary to develop that European spirit in harmony with new conditions. We have a European sense of life, but we are in America, and this fact means that a universal sense of life adaptable to different surroundings must be accomplished in a different way.

If we remove the façade of artificial Europeanism which, in fact, affects but a small group of men—just as architectural influences affect only limited sections of our cities—we come upon the real nucleus of Mexican life, constituted primarily by the middle class, whose whole existence evolves in conformity with European modes of living. Even though Indians make up the greater part of the population, their state of mind has so far prevented them from freeing themselves from nature. Tied to nature, they live in an atmosphere of primitivism that permeates the remainder of the population. Due to its social position, the middle class has been the backbone of our

national history and is still its real substance, in spite of
the fact that it is a minority class. Middle-class concepts
of family, religion, morality, love, and so forth, conform
to the European mold: modified, impoverished, if you
will, but having the effect of vital realities. Therefore,
they can appropriately be considered the product of a
middle-class culture adapted to our geographical surroundings, something we shall identify as *Creole culture*.
Creolism (*criollismo*) is especially prevalent in the cities
of our provinces, which are less inclined to artificiality in
their assimilation of foreign customs. In their spirit as
well as in the faces of their women and in their architecture, these towns preserve a European profile, adapted to
Mexican landscapes. What a magnificent spiritual safe-
guard this would be against the depersonalizing influence of the materialistic metropolis—were it not for the
inertia and passivity of conservatism that neutralize the
provincial virtues!

From this *humus* of generic culture has grown a kind
of selectivity, also creole, that has shown itself in a small
number of personalities. Modest as the latter may seem in
the universal scale of values, we must recognize the fact
that they represent our only tradition of high culture.
The merit of some of these men is due to their persons
rather than their works.

Due to their quality as *men* they have reached the
highest level to which a Hispanic American can aspire.
Their spiritual growth would have been impossible without the nourishment of European culture, which in giving them a more profound consciousness of life has bound
their ideal interests to their native soil. Almost all have
had a relatively significant social impact as educators,

guiding forces, and even exemplary personalities. From time to time their elevated consciences have acted as lightning flashes in the obscure destinies of Hispanic America. Up to the present time, the development of these men in the New World's rarefied atmosphere has been impossible to explain; they have been considered simply as the fruits of a remote European influence. No one ever seems to have realized that this influence would have amounted to nothing, had a heritage from the native land not led to its acceptance. We have seen only one aspect of these figures: their anarchic inclination, their solitary individualism, which seems to have alienated them from all possible cycles of culture. However, from the viewpoint of creolism, all these heterogeneous figures could be placed within one context. Up to now creole culture has not been defined, precisely because its atmospheric existence is omnipresent, yet invisible because of its transparency.

The real motivation for our culture, given the nature of our psychic activity since the time of the Conquest, is religiosity. One must concede that the idea of a unified whole does not preclude struggles of opposing principles; the only basic requirement is that the principles gravitate toward an identical point. In other words, one can say that Mexican history, especially in its spiritual sense, is a matter of the affirmation or negation of religious sentiment. Whichever branch of our ascendancy is considered—that of the Indian or that of the Spanish conqueror—the most notable resultant characteristic is our exalted religiosity. The pioneers of Mexican culture were monks with a mission to fulfill. The Spanish religious will has remained, vigorously embodied in the architecture of our cities. Almost without exception, a church was erected in the center of our towns, or above them on a slope—when the towns were nestled in mountain valleys—so that at any point, near or far, its tower would pull one's line of vision skyward. From a distance, the bell tower and dome of the church are the first visible objects in every small Mexican village; the church silhouette reaches out in linear shadows, as if to give architectural unity to the settlement scattered around it. Not only in a geometric sense is the church the center of its town. Its portal opens out onto a great space called the "plaza of arms," which is the heart of civilian life. Since here one finds the market place, the "governmental palace" and the village park, it is the scene of constant political, religious, and commercial activity—intermingled with all kinds of outdoor pastime. By its great size alone the church seems to have inherited the authority to preside over that human ant hill. However, its importance is often ascribed to its beauty as well. Materially or ideally, the church always occupies a high vantage point.

The real foundation of every culture is a religious sense of life. This sentiment is the energetic core which fires creative activity. It is conceivable that European culture would not have taken root in America if the soldiers who came as conquerors had not been charged with evangelical zeal. Chronologically, the first works of art to appear had a very direct relationship to religious life, and even formed part of it. Church art therefore emerged as Mexico's first expression of Creole culture. Europe had established the basic forms of that art, but it is almost symbolic that the Indian achieved its completion with rock from Mexican soil, and that as he toiled and assembled he occasionally fashioned the ornamental motifs in his own way. First came the ascetic simplicity of the Franciscan style, composed of angles and straight lines that gave the silhouette of each temple the military stamp of a fortress. Its geometric masses outlined by sharp edges and corners symbolize the energetic and almost aggressive masculinity which raised these towers in solitary places above the wilderness. Communities grew up around the churches and an extravagant imagination broke the ascetic discipline, creating a national baroque architecture which revealed a more peaceful and mundane life. And so with time this primitive harshness softened. In its function as the language of religious sentiment, Creole architecture was a living art, which immediately became part of New World life. From a strictly aesthetic point of view, we feel today that other imported styles are out of place next to colonial structures.

Seminaries were the organ of Mexican education from colonial times up to the latter part of the past century. For good or ill, priests were the directors of the people's conscience. It was in the seminaries that through Latin and Greek, the humanities were cultivated. The intellectual formation of several generations followed the norms of Mediterranean culture.[1] Evidently, the kind of instruction then prevailing had not kept up with contemporary European developments. However, neither the Pontifical University nor the schools that formed part of the pedagogical monopoly of the Church were im-

---

[1] Read the *Discourse by Virgil* by Alfonso Reyes (Ed. "Contemporáneos"), from which we quote as follows: "The Mexican spirit endures in the color which Latin waters absorbed from our land after reaching our shores. For three centuries they flowed, continuously bathing the red clays of our soil."

pervious to the modern ideas that mysteriously filtered through official and ecclesiastic censorship. The clamor of the French Revolution resounded too loudly to go unheard in academic cloisters. The first leaders of our war for independence were priests.

The negative phase of Mexico's religiosity begins with the second half of the past century. In its dramatic inception, liberalism brought the revolution of the Reform movement, which resulted in the Constitution [of 1857] and in lay education. But the politicians who instigated and legislated the movement with great Jacobinic passion were intellectuals of a scholastic mentality. What was not rhetoric in their anticlerical polemics was seminary dialectics.

Since that time the temporal power of the Church has been legally nullified, although the impact of that power actually persisted long after its official nullification. Can the same be said about religiosity as a psychological factor of Mexican conduct? The very same free thinkers who achieved the Reform show all the fervor of religious sentiment in the tone of their negations, albeit with a contrary label. By this we mean to say that the Jacobin's psychology is not that of a man idealistically emancipated from religion; it is rather a case of that paradoxical phenomenon recently identified by psychoanalysis as "ambivalent" sentiments. Since the weapons which the free thinkers of 1857 fought with were more rhetorical than philosophical (those men acted as politicians, not as intellectuals), they did not produce an ideological system in which the inverted religious sentiment might appear as an upside-down image on the camera lens. Their "equalitarianism," a vague sort of "humanitarianism," and even their rationalistic attitude, a belated American echo of the French "enlightment," were an inadequate basis for remaking their image of the world. If some conscientious historian of Mexican ideas were ever able to assemble the fragmentary thoughts of these people and to reconstruct the missing data so as to give articulate form to their Jacobinic concept of life, he might well discover its structure to be that of an abstract Catholicism without God, churches, or dogmas.

Like all living organisms, religions die natural deaths. The cause is a slow dissolution of beliefs at the instigation of intellectual criticism, which finds these beliefs incompatible with modern views of life. When religious sentiment grows cold, the external practices and ceremonies of the cult continue by social inertia, like vapid mechanical gestures. At first sight, religious passion seems to be disappearing from the Mexican historical scene; it no longer kindles our spirit. The positivism imported after the Reform movement as a doctrinal support for secular education was the philosophy considered most adequate for eradicating religious ideas. Barreda founded the Preparatory School; its curriculum was established in conformity with Comte's classification of the sciences, in the hope that young people would graduate with new minds. Undeniably, the educational reform succeeded in bringing about a change of orientation which was in keeping with the mentality of our country.

If a destruction of the material power of the Church was an immediate historical necessity, perhaps the same thing could not be said for religious sentiment. Yet the effect of historical events upon individual consciences amounted to an anticlerical argument. Since circumstances did not provide the spiritual stimulus necessary for a radical transformation, religious sentiment was suffocated beneath the weight of those circumstances. Religiosity was not destroyed at that time, even though everyone thought that it had been; it had simply been repressed in the subconscious, owing to inhibitions which took the form of antireligious prejudice. Up to now, the idea of studying the complex mechanisms engendered by the Mexican mind has occurred to no one, despite the fact that it is the only way we can eventually know ourselves. The interpretation of irreligiosity which we are now giving promises a better understanding of many psychological abnormalities of the contemporary Mexican. Religious life is not a transitory phenomenon of the spirit, but a permanent and consubstantial function of its nature. Therefore, when the religious impulse is not applied directly to religious preoccupations, or—more importantly —when its existence is not recognized it becomes an obscure force which corrupts the individual's ability to see things in their proper proportion and forces him to live in an illusory world; this is because he attributes a false magnitude to himself and to things in general.[2] Antireligious intentions lay behind the inclusion of positivism in the program of Mexican education, and in the beginning, positivism and liberalism meant the same thing. There was no doubt that the doctrine in question abounded in points of view favorable to the liberals; in it they found material which was made to order for the rationale of their negations, and these consequently acquired a scientific resemblance and the prestige of modernity. If, in

[2] See Jung, *The Subconscious.*

this pedagogical enterprise, philosophical prudence had prevailed over sectarian passion, it would soon have been obvious that positivism was quite inadequate as a critique of religion, and a far inferior substitute because of its lack of metaphysical meaning. These inherent weaknesses of positivism prevented it from functioning in Mexico as an intellectual corrosive on religious sentiment, but positivism became a mechanically effective form of prejudice against it. Relegated to the lower regions of the soul, the pressure of religious sentiment rises, and, seeking its escape, finds it in scientific superstition. Lacking a religion, the enlightened classes deify science.

On the other hand, the very same religious sentiment —transported upward—gave an idealistic stimulus to Hispanic American thinkers of the late nineteenth century. The most notable among them was José Enrique Rodó, the most complete and the most representative exponent of Creole culture. The great Uruguayan writer also owed a debt to French positivism, that of Comte and Guyau, Taine and Renan; but his positivism had the fullness and nobility of the Renaissance. No one like the ingenious Rodó has succeeded in adapting the most refined European culture to the sensitivity of our race.[3] For the first time the race becomes conscious of a spiritual feeling, symbolized by Rodó in the name of Ariel.

If the youth of America trembled under the bewitch-

---

[3] "Rodó, for all his European qualities—because of them, precisely—is the littérateur who in the purest sense embodies the civilization we are learning about, and the mentality which we are assimilating. He is therefore, so far as correctness and purity are concerned, the writer who best represents us." ("José Enrique Rodó," by Gonzalo Zaldumbide, *Revue Hispanique*, Paris-New York, 1921, p. 13.)

ment of his voice, it was because in the harmony of his
words they discovered themselves and found encourag-
ing formulas for their highest aspirations.

His moderate and luminous literary style, as well as
the Hellenism, Christian spirit, and trust in reason which
his work reveals, were also elements of the Mediterranean
frame of mind. How could this spirit take root in America? These are certainly not things that one can learn in
school, but rather predispositions to sensitivity and understanding which in harmony with certain traditional
forms of expression will color everything that the individual might learn. Only a spiritual power such as the
Catholic Church can give form to these qualities, which,
in turn, give character to the soul: a power which acts
continuously from generation to generation, like an atmosphere which men are compelled to breathe from
birth until death. Catholicism is certainly the vehicle
which implanted in America the classical Mediterranean
mind, unless we ascribe to pure miracle the existence of
personalities like that of Rodó, who in the junglelike
American environment represents a cultural type from
a very different clime. It does not always turn out that
a man who frees himself from his religion also abandons
all its ingredients; on the contrary, in withdrawing his
faith from the supernatural and mythological he retains
its quintessence, i.e., its spiritual sense of life. Rodó's spir-
ituality retained, as far as sentiment was concerned, the
Christian pattern, and, with regard to reason, the universalist ideal transformed into Pan-Americanism. Rodó
takes up Bolívar's idea of the political union of America,
and in a more extensive and less concrete sense he imagines a "magna patria" as the Hispanic American ideal.

It was to be something like a revival of the Ghibelline spirit.

We could cite innumerable examples of similar metamorphoses of religious forms in the works of our greatest writers, but our only purpose is to define in an objective way the elements common to all American culture and undoubtedly, the example already mentioned should suffice. Even though our exposition deals principally with Mexico we have not hesitated to choose a South American writer; the uniformity in historical evolution throughout Hispanic American countries makes conclusions obtained from analysis of an event in one of them applicable to all the rest. Only antireligious prejudice could prevent our seeing that the only common denominator for the capricious individualism of the Hispanic American intelligentsia is religious sentiment.

Whenever an American of great consciousness raises his voice in sincere protestation, religious anxiety arises. Rubén Darío once cried that his soul was the object of contention "between the Cathedral and pagan ruins." Isn't this, perhaps, a valid image of the drama of America? Today very serious problems persist because of the schism between the culture inspired in our cathedrals, and the other, which emanates from *our* ruins. When the two heritages met they could not be combined in the creation of a new synthesis.

As for Mexico, however regrettable the consequences of positivism may ultimately have been for her culture, the doctrine was at one point an element of liberation and progress for the minority in power. It overcame the scholastic stagnation of the seminaries and succeeded in purifying the contaminated air of the schools by opening them to scientific study. Positivism won quick popularity, and its success was due to the fact that it answered a spiritual and social need in Mexico. It was an exotic plant, but in this climate it found oxygen to subsist on, and that is why it lived. It lived almost continuously as a negative passion, in effect contradicting its name of "positivism." But even so, the intensity of its passion converted it into a living dogma; and it should accordingly be considered as a basic phase of Creole culture.

A new element which was in a sense contrary to positivism explains why some enthusiasts expressed their doctrine in lofty, moralizing terms. But because of its naturalistic character, this element was relegated in popular esteem to the status of a common-sense philosophy and a simple justification of instinctive egoism. Such was the origin and substance of the "scientific" moral sense of the increasingly preponderant middle class that enriched itself during Porfirio Díaz' regime.

The cultural mission of the "Athaeneum of Youth" (*Ateneo de la Juventud*), which began in 1908, should be interpreted as a struggle against the demoralization produced by the Porfirian era. This revolutionary intellectual movement preceded the political revolution that broke out two years later.

A precursor of these events was the humanist Justo Sierra, who as professor of history and Minister of Public Education gave inspiration to Mexican cultural life. He was an outstanding man whose forceful personality earned him a place of honor among our most notable minds. The quality of its members and its unity of action made the Athaeneum of Youth a landmark in our history. The vocations of its members were varied. There were humanists like Pedro Henríquez Ureña and philosophers like Antonio Caso and José Vasconcelos; Caso dedicated himself to university teaching, Vasconcelos to political action; there were essayists like Alfonso Reyes, Julio Torri, and Jesús Acevedo; critics like Eduardo Colín; poets like González Martínez.

The Athaeneum was not a cenacle isolated from the world; its purpose was to revive and disseminate culture. All of its members were writers and most of them later became professors at the University. Within the variety of objectives to which each was dedicated lay the common purpose of moral enlightenment. The main problem was to elevate in every possible way the spiritual quality of the Mexican. The Athaeneum assaulted positivism in a campaign to reconstruct the philosophical bases of official education. The race at last gained its spiritual independence from the prejudices that had suppressed it and came to life, unashamed of its name. The Athaeneum philosophers, Caso and Vasconcelos, were aware of the revival of European spiritualism and relied on its most authoritative representatives—Bergson, for example—to bring about an identical movement of ideas in this country. Convinced that higher education had to be founded on philosophy, Caso initiated the teaching of that discipline in the University. In spiritual disciplines—letters, art, philosophy—he emphasized their moral sense.[4] Vasconcelos goes further by expounding a mystic concept of life in which aesthetic sensitivity is the deciding factor. In literature it was also necessary to moralize to writers, showing them how without cultural discipline inspira-

[4] There is a study on the work and personality of Antonio Caso in my book, *Hypothesis*, Mexico, 1928.

tion, and even genius, become sterile. There was a great distance between the rigid aesthetic notions of the Athaeneum of Youth and the Bohemian attitude of the preceding generation of authors, who had collaborated in the *Revista Moderna* of Jesús Valenzuela. For the latter, artistic sense was a matter of ivory towers and artificial paradises. Equally moralizing in tone was the voice of the most prestigious poet of the moment, Enrique González Martínez, who wrote in opposition to the pure aestheticism of Rubén Darío; the intention of his lyric creations is revealed in the following line:

"Twist the neck of the falsely plumed swan."
Moralization also appeared where it is as indispensable as aesthetic sense—in literary criticism. Eduardo Colín possessed both of these qualities.

In general, the work of the Athaeneum amounted to a shaking up of the sleepy apathy of Mexico's intellectual world. It propagated new ideas, awoke curiosity and uneasiness, and extended the conventional view on the problems of culture. By philosophical means it tended to counteract the growing influence of utilitarianism, instilling young people with sensitivity for spiritual values. The effect of that agitation during the decade which begins in 1910 was to heighten the tone and widen the radius of our intellectual life. So far no one has emphasized the fact that this intellectual resurgence takes place in an atmosphere of tragedy. It was in 1910, precisely, that the Revolution broke out. Civil war did not spread simultaneously throughout the country; it was rather like a traveling whirlwind that upset everything in its way; but immediately after its conclusion life became normal. However, the consequences of war were quickly felt everywhere in the country. No one could escape the increasingly grave economic crises.

One can read the works of the philosophers, men of letters, and poets, without finding a word of disillusionment, or a shade of radical pessimism, or of any kind of negation. Our thinkers adhere enthusiastically to every philosophy that energetically affirms life in terms of its spiritual values and move closer to an acceptance of life's religious sense. Their voice is that of the Hispanic-American race, whose intellectual tradition is a variation on the theme of spiritualism. When Vasconcelos gives the University its motto, "By virtue of my race the spirit shall speak," his thought seems to obey a suprapersonal will. He speaks as one inspired, and one whose intuition suddenly illuminates the mysteries of the collective subconscious.

The enlightened quality of this intellectual work was possible because of the free development it enjoyed, detached from Mexico's immediate realities; however, its authors do not fail to achieve a certain heroic stature. Popular criticism has denied this work its national significance, failing to find in it sufficient concern with contemporary Mexican history. But ultimately every intellectual became aware of the fact that his immediate reality was death. He also discovered that in defending his faith, his reservoir of culture, he was also defending life. He was therefore not alienated from his world, because his salvation of himself contributed in some degree to the salvation of his country.

Neither scorn of country, nor incomprehension of his problems have led the Mexican intellectual to omit reference to his environment. He has discovered, rather, that when his spirit demands expression, it must do so in an appropriate language which America has not yet created, and which only European culture can provide. Our "Europeanism" is not always a frivolous adherence to fashion, or a servile mimetism; it is also an appreciation of the effective values of human life and the desire to enter the world which contains them. To be indifferent to this world would perhaps constitute a sign of inferiority that would condemn us to permanent imprisonment within national horizons, and that would prevent us from ever approaching a greater community of men. Ideally, this has been Europe's pretense, so as to monopolize universal culture in the modern age. Fortunately, the Hispanic American is capable of rising to a spiritual sense of the universal, and, within possibility, has the will to do so. We have already shown that this will is to be found in the expression of our most highly esteemed thinkers and that it is a *leit motiv* of Creole culture. Even if Vasconcelos' doctrine of the "cosmic race" is not a believable prophecy (it is, in effect, an ideal quite out of proportion with the present state of *our* life and its possibilities), we can discern in that idea an abstraction of its content, a mythological expression of the universalist will of *our race*.

Driven by the need for a superior culture and failing to find it in the world around them, a select group of Mexicans found it inside themselves. They were the soul of Mexico, but a soul—without a body. In order to sustain itself, a superior culture needs some social form of a median culture which constitutes its vital atmosphere. This would be the body which has been lacking and which is necessary to accomplish the organic totality of our culture and make it work. Only when enlightenment becomes available to the community as a whole will the spirit of the cultured minority reach everywhere, and activate the people as the nervous system activates the various parts of a vital organism.

V.
The "Abandonment of Culture" in Mexico

The predominant philosophy in Mexico at the beginning of the twentieth century was positivism, and although it may have been interpreted differently by the common man and by the "scientist," it was essentially the same notion. The Athaeneum of Youth launched its campaign against positivistic utilitarianism and materialism. Its members were the elite of the Mexican intelligentsia. They attempted to rejuvenate the intellectual atmosphere by introducing a new idealistic philosophy that would rehabilitate the spiritual values that had been so degraded in Mexico under the influence of positivism. The cultural mission of the Athaeneum was animated by the same spirit as was Rodó's *Ariel*. Within a short time the orientation of philosophical teaching at the University changed. The authority of Comte and Spencer ceded to that of Bergson, James, Boutroux, and others. The new climate of ideas excited the young people and awoke in them an enthusiasm for the transcendent problems of culture; but this enthusiasm soon burned out.

When Vasconcelos began his work in public education in 1919, a fundamental change took place in our cultural destiny. In its simplest terms, Vasconcelos' program provided for an extensive elementary education which no one—to then—had fought for as a form of social justice. His program materialized, then, as a revolution in education which incited a critical revision at all levels of instruction. The result was the emergence of several reforms which affected everything from the primary schools up through the University. At that time also a sense of nationalism was being born. Interest in secondary and technical education was strong. At first university studies were looked down upon; later came the idea of placing them at the service of the people. The fact that this attitude emanated from different sources—from educators, politicians, and intellectuals—and that it was shared by young people and the masses, proves that the movement was more than artificial. It was not even necessary to explain it and reinforce it with theories. The fact that from the start its existence seemed logical to every-

one was another reason for affirming its historical necessity, and for recognizing that its aims were not intellectual. Even though the new tendencies seemed heterogeneous, they actually had more than one point in common.
In their dissatisfaction with traditional educational principles, and also in their appreciation of the merits of instruction with a view to utility and quantity, they all
coincided. This was evident. The validity of higher education had not yet been questioned. Up until 1920 its
value had never been disputed; after that it became an
object of controversy. Since that year, interest in university studies has declined; university men themselves consider them to be of less importance than formerly. Also
lost, though not entirely, is respect for the "intellectuals"
and envy of them. In Mexico we have witnessed, in this
instance spontaneously and with no trace of imitation,
the recurrent phenomenon accurately described by Curtius as the "abandonment of culture."

There is no doubt that the common denominator of
pedagogical reforms is *useful action*. Students, teachers,
even intellectuals, show their eagerness to acquire knowledge *immediately* applicable to life. For this reason,
"pragmatism" and "vitalism" have been the doctrines
most highly regarded in our university circles. By comparing these academic phenomena with others which
have occurred outside the cultural realm, we can appreciate the psychological origin of the developments we
have just described.

Even a superficial examination of our social environment reveals that Mexican life everywhere has been devoted to the attainment of immediate results. Programs
for individual and collective living are devised for the

present, or for the immediate future. It matters little that reality does not respond satisfactorily to the impatience to relieve human need; the intention is the important thing. This unrealistic attitude gives the impression of thoughtless activity, with no definite goal, and with all the characteristics of instinctive conduct. These new projects for national education, and the vague notions of the meaning of culture in which they seek justification, reflect the ideals of the collective state. Their inspiration does not come from the upper regions of the mind, but rather from the dark depths of instinct. But such an origin is no reason for calling the projects inferior or unworthy. Historically effective movements grow out of the human soul, in which the primordial impulses of life dwell. Mexican educational reform comes as an expression of a people's vital drive to affirm and justify its existence, and also as the reflection on a cultural level of a social transformation which has brought the masses to the forefront of public life. In society the masses perform the same role that instinct plays in the individual being.

At the beginning of our century there was a general and pronounced disdain among Mexicans for everything domestic; their interests were concentrated abroad, especially Europe, in order to find models which could give them a superior sense of life. No one would embark on a new enterprise without first acquainting himself with what the Europeans had done in similar cases. Spiritually, Mexico was a colonial country. The supreme ideal of the Mexican bourgeois was to go to Europe and receive his education in its schools and universities, and frequently he never returned. Men were reluctant to accept the fact that they had been born in this part of the planet;

and although circumstances forced them to remain physically in Mexico, their spirit lived in Europe.

During the second decade of this century a change
took place in the Mexican's attitude toward the world. He
now began to take interest in his own life and in his immediate surroundings. In his own country he discovered
values which he had not seen before, and at that same
moment his appreciation for Europe began to diminish,
precisely when it was involved in the terrible years of
war. As a result of this spectacle many Hispano-Ameri-
cans lost their illusions about the culture they had so
greatly admired. Afterwards came postwar pessimism,
which even further weakened the authority Europe held
over American thought. Spengler's spectacular book, *The
Decline of the West*, provided the first philosophical arguments against European culture. These attacks seemed to
confirm Mexican attitudes, which were already in instinctive conflict with the overseas spirit.

What was the cause of these psychological changes?
Sudden consciousness of the national ego (*el yo*) had, in
the case of Mexico, a biological origin. Failure in numerous attempts to imitate a foreign civilization has taught
us the slow and painful lesson that we have a character of
our own and a unique destiny which can no longer be
ignored. Out of the new national sentiment comes the
will to form a new culture of our own in opposition to the
European. In order to give the cold shoulder to Europe,
Mexico has resorted to nationalism—which is itself a European trait.

It was natural that Mexicans should feel resentment
against Europe, since their dependence on its spirit had
for centuries caused them to belittle national values. Fas-

cination with Europe was often the reason for abandoning domestic traditions. But unfortunately, the new interest in things national has not had a clear objective, and, moreover, the good intention of determining our own destiny is mixed with hostility toward European virtues. The reason is simply resentment. Many weak personalities took advantage of circumstances in which culture was underrated so as to rid themselves of the obligation to culture, the attainment of which called for serious effort. At first, nationalism was an empty gesture with no other purpose than the negation of everything European. The result was that Mexico became isolated from the civilized world, willfully depriving itself of fertile spiritual influences, without which the development it so ardently desired was not possible.

The task of giving our way of life a characteristic stamp lacked the point of departure it logically should have had: knowledge of the Mexican man. Until his character, his desires, his capabilities, and his historical vocation are defined, all projects for reviving the nationalist sense will be blind attempts doomed to failure. An unclear notion of the Mexican way of being has given rise to two schools of thought that passionately dispute the question of what norms should guide Mexican culture; they are the "nationalists" and the "Europeanizers." I have reached conclusions that differ equally from both these ways of viewing the problem.

The nationalists are wrong in opposing Mexico's participation in universal culture and in trying, thereby, to isolate it from the rest of the world. Undoubtedly any such isolation, instead of nurturing the development of an original spirit, may well have the contrary effect and impede absolutely all forms of spiritual life, original or not. Furthermore, it is dangerously audacious to search deliberately for an original style, because being original or unoriginal is the result of a destiny in which the conscious will cannot participate.

On the other hand, the Europeanizers are wrong in failing to consider European culture from the Mexican viewpoint; instead, they see Mexico from the viewpoint of Europe. They are men who idealistically abandon the life around them and cease being Mexicans. Their spirit is devoid of that native element which upon undergoing the influence of European culture grafts onto the tree of the latter a new branch, one that will later became an independent cultural unit.

II

It is the Iberian stamp—Spanish or Portuguese—that has had the strongest effect in determining the character of the people and the climate of life in Latin America. The *elite*, at least up to now, have sought their intellectual culture in France. But now one senses the increasing influence of North America in the organization of the material aspects of existence and its growing technical complexities.[1]

In the specific case of Mexico we can say that the North American ideal of life has been rapidly replacing the European norms which once prevailed. Practicality, money, machines, and speed are the thing which provoke the greatest enthusiasm in modern men.

The guiding principle of Mexican education today is what we could call by way of image the *instrumental conception of man*. Individual instruction aimed at tech-

---

[1] A. Siegfried, *Amérique Latine*, p. 143.

nical specialization and even professional careers can have no other result. Only a certain biological sense of urgency has impelled us to accept in this country the instrumental kind of culture prevalent in the United States, where every level of introduction from elementary school through college is arbitrarily governed by principles of technical skill. No one is personally responsible for the change of orientation in Mexican education; it was due rather to the example set by the materially brilliant civilization which lives next to us and which makes the spectacle of our poverty all the more desolate. Some ironic destiny seems to have brought into contiguity a country of luxurious vitality, where there is an excess of everything that the most fabulous ambition can imagine, and that other country, where only nature is clothed in splendor and filled with power, where man is virtually naked and enjoys no protection other than a merciful climate.

North American pedagogy is unconsciously seasoned with a mechanistic concept of society, which is an abbreviation of the cosmic view that imagines the world as a machine. The mechanistic system is the formula by which a man of instinct would try to set things in order. For such a man the world is a prey to be tamed and governed as easily as he controls his machines. In technical specialization, as in the very precise acts of instinctive animals, there are pre-existing solutions for a limited number of typical cases, and these must be invariable. For this reason the technician is fit to live only in very special situations. He remains, if you will, a victim of his rigid specialty; for him there is only one circumstance in life. Placed in any other situation, the specialist is lost.

Instinct without some degree of sublimation, i.e., instinct permitted to act in its purely natural state, is simply brute force. In such cases its biological function is inverted, and instead of being a life-giving source, it becomes a force that destroys life. When instinct inspires material civilization, it sacrifices the authentic life of man for a false one, composed of automatism and mechanization. If schooling is good only for the instruction of material techniques, that means it is preparing individuals to be devoured all the more easily by civilization. This is indeed a monstrous concept of schooling. In contrast, education must be thought of as the vigor of life itself, fighting off a civilization which by converting men into foolproof automatons creates the illusion that it has adequately prepared them for life—though without will, or intelligence, or feeling. In short, without a soul.

VI.
The Profile
of Mexican
Culture

In one of his observations on the New World, Bolívar wrote that we Americans are Europeans by heritage. In Mexico this heritage was abused for an entire century; there was excessive imitation of Europe, with no other guide than individual caprice. The original sin of Mexican Europeanism was its lack of a standard for selecting foreign seeds of culture which in our spiritual earth could have produced the appropriate remedies for particular needs. That standard should have been none other than reality itself, but reality was unknown, because all our attention and interest had turned to Europe. The fallacy of always attempting to imitate Europe was possibly derived from an erroneous concept of culture which by extravagant idealization separated it from life, as if warmth and energy were not indispensable to the spirit's survival.

The prevailing culture—present or future—is necessarily that which determines vocation of the race and its historical destiny. We shall try to draw the profile of a culture that conceivably could exist in Mexico, given certain organic circumstances of society and man as the results of a particular history.

We must not continue to practice a false Europeanism; but it is just as urgent to avoid another dangerous illusion, cherished by an equally false type of Mexicanism. Enlivened by a resentment against everything foreign, this Mexicanism seeks to rebuild our national life on other bases than those which it has had up to now—as if it were possible to undo in one moment our entire history. There is an attempt to isolate Mexico from all contact with the outside world so as to free its native qualities from all extraneous elements. Just as "Europeanism" was founded on the ideal of a culture which could exist apart from life, "nationalism" was founded on the belief that Mexico was already complete in itself, with a definitive national physiognomy, and that its only need was to be drawn out into the light of day, like an unearthed idol. Such a belief is supported by an inclination to the picturesque—mountain scenes, dotted with Indian figures in their typical white cotton suits and with cactus plants.

Recent art has undertaken an amplification—as in a resounding box—of the "picturesque" dimensions that have found wide acceptance, especially among Yankee tourists. But this Mexico of the *charro* (Mexican horseman) and the Mexico of the *china poblana* (colorful style of women's regional dress), as well as the Mexico of the legendary savage (whose novelty and attraction for Europeans I cannot understand; there is proof of their own savagery in what has transpired since 1914), constitute a Mexico for export which is just as false as the romantic Spain of the tambourine.

But if we can rid our nationalistic spirit of all its resentment against things foreign (the kind of resentment which is typical in those suffering from an inferiority complex), there will undoubtedly remain a moral substance of absolute value for Mexico. This will be the voice of our most authentic being, which now finally makes itself heard after so many years in which the Mexican turned a deaf ear to his destiny. It is almost impossible to believe that this is a novelty; but it is. Mexicans have not lived naturally; their history has always lacked candor. That is why they now should quickly heed that voice, which demands a life of sincerity. We must have the courage to be ourselves and the humility to accept the life that fate bestowed upon us without being ashamed of its poverty. All the ills that have outlived us are due to our failure to practice these simple rules of austerity; we have chosen to feign a situation which is very superior to that in which we actually live. Many of the sufferings which now afflict us will disappear the day we cure ourselves of our vanity. As a consequence of living outside the reality of our being, we are lost in a chaotic world, in the midst of which we walk blindly and aimlessly, buffeted about by the four winds. For times of radical confusion there is no better remedy than to withdraw into ourselves, to return to the native soil. There is no doubt that after periods of muddled thinking and debilitation men and even entire peoples have revived. In our particular case, a figurative return to our own land will give us the physical and moral health necessary for recovering confidence in the future. It is a consolation to note that for some years the Mexican conscience has steadfastly sought true national introspection. But unfortunately the examination of our conscience has not been undertaken with the rigor, depth, and objectivity that the case requires. How can people be impartial judges in questions which affect their personal interests and partisan passions? Human experience shows that an interest or a passion cannot be defeated except by a greater interest or a greater passion. Therefore, we shall be incapable of knowing ourselves as individuals or as a people until we can overcome our little passions with the great passion for truth. This is one of the ways of disinterested love for persons and things, whether real or ideal. Love of knowledge was best symbolized by the *eros* of Plato. In order to develop, this love of knowledge must become a fundamental concern of Mexican education.

The man who has this passion for truth will have also the indispensable moral strength to carry out a merciless analysis of himself, overcoming the weaknesses that might prevent a clear and objective view of his interior world. But the achievement of his high mental vantage point, from which we can look at things not as if we were extraterrestrial beings, but merely intelligent spectators, would not suffice to probe the inner recesses of reality. To this moral discipline an intellectual discipline must be added. It would be senseless to insist on this point if there were not a trend of opinion obviously favorable to scientific learning as the absolute prerequisite for an investigation of Mexican problems. A false concept of science seems to support this dangerous error.

Indeed, it is an exceedingly vulgar concept, the result of ignorance of superficiality, in which one can hear the distant echo of positivism; it is the fallacy that knowledge is acquired simply by opening up the five senses to reality. In this way of thinking, the intellectual function becomes subservient to the scientific process, to the extent that experience by its own virtue has the magic capacity of converting itself into ideas. Scientific research is reduced to a matter of accumulating facts, as if gathering them up to a certain amount were sufficient to cause scientific knowledge to burst into light. The chauvinistic mentality supposes, since science is European, that all intellectual preparation must constitute a bias in the scholar's mind, and accordingly blinds him to its native originality.

Therefore it is not surprising that such a theory of science should encourage the notion of creating a "Mexican science" which would admit no debt to the principles of universal science.

This is why in Mexico the true theory of science must be assimilated, because the popularized image that we have just described is no more than its caricature. Scientific research is impracticable if it does not confront reality with a prejudgment. Prejudgment is what guides the attention toward a given phenomenon; to prejudg-

ment we owe our discovery of the relationship among
different facts and perceive the continuity of a single
process in events of diverse appearance. In a word, prejudgment is what within the medium of experience leads
us to the scientific idea. But one cannot acquire these pre-
judgments without learning, before the actual investigation, the principles of the science in question.

To believe that we can develop in Mexico an original
culture unrelated to the rest of the world constitutes a
total misunderstanding of what culture is. The commonest notion is that culture is pure *knowledge*. One fails to
recognize the truth that it is rather a function of the spirit
destined to humanize reality. But it is clear that this function is not spontaneous. Education, then, develops in the
mind of each individual the wealth of culture already ac-
cumulated. Once that education is properly oriented, it
should not simply work toward an increase in knowledge,
but toward the transformation of the latter into a spiritual
capacity to comprehend and elaborate the substance of
every meaningful experience. Only by extracting from
traditional culture its most subtle essence and making it
a basic element of our spirit, can we speak of an "assimilation of culture."

Each spirit needs for its development the support and
stimulus of a universal culture. It is therefore evident
that the good intention of examining Mexican conscience
may come to naught if we isolate it from the outside
world, closing our doors to every possible foreign influence, for then we shall be left in the dark. The two extreme options in educational method are equally injuri-
ous to the future of national culture. One is to ignore
Mexican reality altogether, which is what happened dur-

ing the past century, so as to obtain a European culture
at the possible cost of destroying our own ideas. The other
is to deny categorically the significance of European culture, in the utopian hope of creating a Mexican culture
which of course could not grow out of nothing. We shall
never be able to decipher the mysteries of our being unless we can illuminate its depths with a guiding ideal
that can come only from Europe.

When we reach some understanding of the idiosyncra-
cies of our national soul, we will have a standard to guide
us through the complexities of European culture—which
contains many important elements that are of no interest
to us. Only by scientific knowledge of the Mexican mind
will we have a basis for a systematic exploration of the
maze of European culture and a separation of those elements which can be assimilated to our environment. Up
to now, fashion has been the only arbiter for evaluating
the heterogeneous products of spiritual life in the Old
World. Lacking precise data on the nature of our soul, we
have also lacked reference points for acquiring a Mexican perspective of European phenomena. The idea of selecting conscientiously and methodically the forms of
European culture potentially adaptable to our own environment has never occurred to us. There is no doubt
that such a system is possible, on the basis of choosing
certain instinctive affinities that persuade our race to prefer certain cultural aspects over others. The hard thing
is to distinguish between genuine congenialities and certain misguided interests which have nevertheless drawn
our attention to culture. With the exception of an insignificant minority, Mexicans up to now have not cared
about getting to the bottom of culture; instead, they have

been content to stand aside, dazzled by its brilliant outward effects.

In the future Mexico must have a Mexican culture, but we have no illusions about its being original or unique. By Mexican culture we mean universal culture made over into *our own*, the kind that can coexist with us and appropriately express our spirit. Curiously enough, the only way open to us—in order to shape this Mexican culture—is to continue learning about European culture. Our race is a branch of a European race. Our history has unfolded in a European manner. But we have not succeeded in forming our own culture, because we have separated culture and life. We no longer want an artificial culture that lives like a hothouse flower; we do not want a false Europeanism.

It is therefore essential to approach our problem in that modern spirit which by reiteration has become trite: to relate culture to life. As far as scientific knowledge is concerned, it is necessary to correlate continually the study of universal scientific principles with a specific analysis of our own reality. One reason for the hostility toward culture is the Mexican's individualistic character, resistant to all authority and to every standard. Accordingly, to accept the idea of radical "nationalism" would be tantamount to perpetuating the spiritual crisis; it would mean taking the path of least resistance, so as to continue facile achievements, superficial observations, and fragmentary studies devoid of scientific rigor. To give substance to our spiritual work of the future, it will be necessary to prepare our young people in schools and universities by means of an austere program basically oriented toward discipline of the will and intelligence. Concrete knowledge is what should least concern us with regard to culture. The critically important thing for Mexico now is to glean from culture as much as it can of intellectual and moral discipline. When this is achieved it will be possible to show that even those who reach the highest pinnacles of spiritual life need not, in their haughtiness, succumb to the error of rejecting native values. On the contrary, their enlightenment will permit them to comprehend and judge Mexican life more effectively.

VII.
The Profile
of Man

The destiny of culture in Mexico, which has been the theme of our investigation, demands scrutiny of the Mexican's spiritual future, because both the origin and the fulfillment of culture reside in man. We cannot even imagine a culture whose principles were indifferent to human aims. The ideas we are now about to present on the theme of our cultural destiny are based on this assumption, which should be self-evident. "Culture," says Max Scheler, "is not 'education for something,' not *for* a profession, specialty, or product of any specific kind; nor does culture lend itself to the attainment of such purposes. Rather, every sort of training 'for something' exists for the sake of culture, for the sake of *the perfect man.*" The ultimate goal of the spirit is not culture but the development of human personality. That cultural product is a station on the road along which the soul travels in its endeavor for self-discovery. For this reason the personal influence of educated men is much more efficient as a cultural stimulus in general than as a stimulus for the achievement of specific works.

In order to find out what possibilities for a Mexican culture exist, it is first necessary to know the spiritual circumstances of those intellectual leaders who are going to develop it. Most will agree that there is a sore need for great intellectuals who, gifted with a clear awareness of our unique historical destiny, could set our course amidst the chaos. Mexicans distinguished for their ability and refinement are of an uprooted type; that is, they have not deigned to concern themselves with Mexican life, which they consider devoid of all dignity. So far as thought is concerned, the cultured minority express the individualism of the race, but their thought and literary action have traditionally been indifferent to the history of their country. When an exception occurs and some writer consents to address the nation in authoritative tones, he speaks in abstractions that might apply to any country or time.

On the other side of the fence are the radical nationalists, who are usually poorly educated men, with no culture whatsoever. They see things superficially, through a narrow provincialism which makes them believe that the Mexican essence is local color. If their influence ever got the upper hand in the spiritual life of Mexico, the model man of culture would have a small-town mentality and would soon reduce his country's significance to the level of an inconsequential village, lost in the midst of the civilized world. Just as it should turn away from a universalist type of culture without roots in Mexico, our capital city should reject all picturesque Mexicanism lacking universality. The ideal yet to be achieved, we might say, is personality subjected to a formula which could harmonize the specific values. A better example of what we mean is Russian and Spanish art, in which the artist succeeds in reproducing the most individualistic traits of his race at the point where his work attains universal transcendence. The norm of "nationalism" should be a purification of our own kind of life without obstructing its participation in the universal realm.

The time has come for Mexico to bring forth the fruits of its personality. And since it has not yet produced any, should we assume that our country is actually sterile? No, the causes are quite different. The fact is that a number of historical accidents have distorted our life, leading Mexicans astray in their psychological evolution. Personal development in school and society has not adhered to a conscientious and reflective discipline; the necessary atmosphere of peace and tranquillity has been missing. The formation of our character over the centuries has been an erratic process, activated by subconscious drives. The result of these abnormalities is that our destiny has been obscured, and today we march confusedly, striving to find the true direction of our existence.

But one omen on the horizon gives us confidence in Mexico's future: our people are now aware of the void within them and they have awakened to a desire to fill it, forming thereby the personality which they lack. Unfortunately not everyone is convinced that the problem of our culture is not so much in creating works as in forming men. "Public consciousness," if indeed it exists, should sense that the solution of that problem is an urgent moral necessity.

To accomplish this it is first necessary to free Mexicans from the subconscious complexes which up to now have thwarted the growth of their real selves. It would be naive to think that human conduct is determined by its most apparent causes. More often than one might suspect, man does not know what he wants and ignores the real sources of his action. One needs a certain degree of psychological knowledge in order to explore successfully those unconscious drives which disturb the conscious faculties, exciting the imagination, twisting one's judgment, weakening one's sense of values, and finally bringing about permanent mental changes in people most susceptible to those mysterious forces. I do not speak here of pathological phenomena, but of psychic processes which occur daily in the lives of an incredible number of normal and healthy men. Contemporary psychology has carefully examined the nature of these processes and discovered truths; this priceless technique for analyzing and understanding man in his private and public activities is a guide for research on historical and social topics. Today's thinker is thus able to gain a penetrating view of the soul, and to discover the unknown subterranean world in whose depths history begins and later unfolds in the full light of day.

Elsewhere we have tried to apply these principles to an interpretation of certain social facts in our culture. We have also made several fundamental observations induced from a psychoanalysis of the Mexican, studied not in his individual structure but in his role as a member of a political community. In that part of our study the most important elements of the Mexican subconscious are listed. I shall only add that it is easy to destroy such harmful complexes, for they are the result of unjust comparisons with European standards. If the Mexican has a depressive idea of his worth, it is because he has value judgments which, as one might expect, vary in importance from one moment to another. Comparisons need not be made with men in other countries or at other levels of culture. Ideally each man should think out his potential qualities to their maximum perfection, and so obtain the best possible idea of his capabilities. This preliminary model will be the Mexican's yardstick, the indispensable standard for his self-esteem. Then the values manifested will be intrinsic in character, and measurable only by the greater or smaller distance between what has actually been done and what it was possible to do; but their status will be unaffected by comparison with the values of other civilizations.

When these depressive complexes vanish, our false character will automatically disappear. Like a disguise, it has covered the Mexican's authentic way of being as a compensation for his painful feelings of inferiority. That day will be the beginning of our second War of Independence, which may turn out to be more transcendental than the first, because it will free the spirit for the fulfillment of its own destiny.

When the Mexican escapes the bonds of his subconscious limitations, it will be possible to say that he has learned to analyze his soul. It will then be time to begin a new life under the constellation of sincerity, because, as Rubén Darío says, "To be sincere is to be powerful." This elementary precept, so simple in theory, is quite difficult in practice. Innumerable factors work relentlessly against the affirmation of one's individuality: social expediency, vanity, fear, egoism, evil passions, and so on. All these factors confuse the mind and lead to an erroneous choice of moral guides. One dangerous attitude in Mexico is the belief that an authentic national type already exists; and, in its diametrical opposition to Europeanism, this belief will inevitably lead to a reaffirmation of false Mexicanism. The best way to avoid mistakes is to remember that there is no such thing as a model for Mexican life. We must live without prejudice, always ready to identify the phenomena that rise spontaneously from within—in order to distinguish them from those other impulses which, though residing *within* us, are not part of us. The only standard in this case is a well-balanced intuition that leads us to distinguish between what is our own and what is somebody else's. The most serious threat to the ultimate satisfaction of our will is a kind of civilized artificiality. This is why we must begin with some degree of primitive innocence, without worrying too much about where we are going to end up. Only thus will characteristic nuances begin to appear, enabling us to distinguish ourselves from the other peoples of the world. One might say that in order to achieve the ideal of sincerity it is first necessary to cure our obsession for originality, and to take inspiration instead from a prodigious will to perfection. This is the surest way to cast some light over the problem of our destiny.

The ideological confusion in which we have lived in recent decades has caused us to abandon the notion of humanism in Mexico. Therefore, if we want to satisfy the new will which has just been born, we must set a *humanistic* course for education. "Over the word humanism," says Curtius, "hovers the scholarly dust of four centuries." Nevertheless, humanism is here to stay, because its spirit is not bound within the limits of any particular historical era, such as Antiquity or the Renaissance; rather, it transcends the past and reaches out to all periods. To be a partisan of humanism in these times is not to be a conservative who longs to return to antiquity. Every historical moment has its own humanism, and in every historical moment humanistic inspirations of the past can be seen in a new perspective.

Culture in Mexico has always tended to learning from experience—from consummated truths—but without repeating the vital process necessary for their attainment. For this reason culture has not been an effective agent in promoting the spirit; that is, it has not been "humanistic." Our studies would undoubtedly acquire some humanistic meaning if—without actually changing the content of instruction—we were to give less emphasis to erudite information and more to an exercise of the functions that have led to culture. This idea is more easily understood if we apply to culture the distinction which Spinoza makes between *natura naturata* and *natura na-*

turans: between culture already objectified in works and culture in action. Culture in action must be the principal goal of higher education in Mexico.

We are so oblivious to the concept of humanism that the word is strange to our ears, as if it no longer belonged to this age. But that impression notwithstanding, the essence of humanism is quite compatible with modern life; what is more, it is indispensable to give it the depth which it has lost. Curtius says:

To grasp the intimate meaning of humanism, let us conduct an intellectual experiment. Let us suppose that social and scientific progress has reached its height. Imagine a society without war, without class struggles, without any struggle for existence. Social and sexual problems have been solved. Sickness has disappeared and the prisons are closed. There are no governmental or economic restrictions. Production increases without obstructions. The terrors of death have been eradicated by officially approved euthanasia. In this ideal society there is nothing for socialism to do, nor for pacifism, nationalism, or imperialism. In this society, however, men will continue to be born and to die. All the technical problems of society are solved; the only problem remaining is this: to find out the meaning of human existence. How should I live? How should I love? How should I die? These questions will always be asked and perhaps now with more anxiety than ever. This utopian man, who exists in the best of all possible worlds, will wonder in anguish and sorrow: What am I? What is humanity? How can we make life into something more radiant and profound?

"But," Curtius adds, "it's unnecessary to await this imaginary humanity of the future. Those questions persist today just as they have persisted throughout history, because they are questions born with the being and nature of man." Fiction has made it possible to see that humanism does not belong exclusively to any given epoch of the past, that its essence is, as it were, extratemporal.

Although the need for this humanistic culture is evident, its general acceptance will be difficult to obtain, for it is bound to clash with a strong and deeply-rooted prejudice in the Mexican conscience: that of practical education. Mexico has not escaped the universal epidemic of mechanistic civilization, and as we shall soon see, there is a very strong temptation to let it thrive here. Evolution toward modernity has already begun in Mexican life. As one might suppose, this has had repercussions in the field of culture, which has changed its direction in order to prepare the technicians required by new ways of life. Despite the fact that the work of transformation is still in its incipient phase, there is already evidence of those grave contradictions inherent to modern civilization and characteristic of the most advanced countries in a world on the brink of crisis.

Owing to some demoniacal force within them, the creations of man—once they have left his hand—become autonomous and, in obedience to a logic of their own, continue their unobstructed development with results entirely free of the author's original intention. Thus something designed as a simple means of serving man, such as modern technology, permeates all in exorbitant proportions; by its own dynamism it has become an end in itself. The objects created by civilization accumulate in infinite number—a process which the human will is helpless to stop—to the point of exerting an adverse effect on man, who, no longer needing those objects, nevertheless remains subjected to them, like a spider caught in the strands of its own web. Far from benefiting man, the monstrous phenomenon of mechanistic civilization has turned into a heavy burden which is all the more dangerous because it threatens his destruction. Awed by the power of the machines he has invented, man has forgotten his own purposes and exalts instead the mechanical ideal which he would like to see realized in society and in individual life. The growing complication of contemporary life has made it necessary to disperse human activity among a multitude of specializations which draw the person away from his life. Man seems unaware of the true destiny of things as he loses himself in a complacent acceptance of the new technology. It is a frequent occurrence, even in the realm of art.

Our contemporary civilization is the gigantic instrument of a will to power which, ever since the Renaissance, has been man's motivating force. By means of scientific techniques he has victoriously extended his domination over nature, but, on the other hand, he has not been able to dominate the demoniacal force of the instruments themselves. In ever-increasing quantities these have imprisoned man in their overwhelming mass. When the Mexican's character becomes reasonable there is no doubt that his will to power, which today is his most salient feature (though inconsequential as a compensation for the Mexican's depressive notion of himself), will diminish to a considerable degree. Spengler is right in saying that modern technology is not a natural necessity for the colored races: "Only Faustian Man thinks, feels, and lives in its forms. For him that technology is a *spiritual* necessity."[1] There is no doubt that the white sector

[1] *Man and Technology*, p. 124.

of the Mexican population to some extent understands
and feels the same way as "Faustian man" does. But this
is not the case with the indigenous part of the population.
Men who in Mexico have tried to solve the problem of
civilizing the Indians have believed it possible to adapt
them to modern technology, with the idea that it is universal and that any man in possession of his rational faculties can utilize it. They fail to see that to *understand*
modern technology is not sufficient reason for adopting
it; that it is essential, also, to have the same spirit as that
of the men who created it. Jung, the psychologist, tells
that a friend of his—a Pueblo Indian chieftain—told
him: "We don't understand the whites. They always
want something; they are always restless, always search-
ing for something. What do they seek? We don't know.
We can't understand them. Their noses are sharp, their
lips, thin and cruel; their faces have pronounced features.
We think they are all crazy."

Like the Pueblos, Mexican Indians are psychologically
incapable of accepting technology, because, for reasons
that we need not examine here, they lack the will to
power; they do not belong to the race of rapacious men.
An Indian can learn how to drive an automobile, or to
operate a farm tractor, but he is not likely to experience
the white man's emotion in contemplating the prodigious
work-capacity that these instruments contain. Therefore,
since no natural need impels the Indian to seek that superior technology, he abandons it and falls back on his
primitive methods—as long as no external compulsion
forces him to continue in civilization.

It is quite evident that the colored races do not possess
the spirit to dominate. If the Mexican has no marked will

to power, in the sense of primordial psychic force, then the most convincing reason for him to establish modern civilization in his country is to have a means of defense against the dominating races, by using their own weapons against them. For "men of color," says Spengler, "technology is no more than a weapon in the struggle against Faustian civilization, a weapon similar to a branch of a tree which is thrown away as soon as it has served its purpose."[2] According to the same thinker, a *struggle of races* has been going on for several centuries, and since World War I it has become just as important as the *struggle of classes*, and perhaps more so. It is so extensive and so acute that it has reached the proportions of a "world racial revolution." It is a war of colored men, who have multiplied everywhere, against their master, the white man. Now the struggle is beginning to use the arms of technical knowledge, a kind of premium available in books and in institutions of higher learning. The white man has committed the error of betraying his own civilization, giving out the secret of technology and placing in his enemy's hands an instrument which, according to Spengler, may destroy Faustian civilization itself. He believes that the struggle of races in Latin America begins with the Independence movements:

The independence movement in Spanish America from the time of Bolívar (1811) on, would have been inconceivable without the Anglo-French literature of 1770, without the example of Napoleon, or without the revolutionary movement of North America against England. At first the struggle was exclusively between white groups: the aristocratic Creole landowners, established several generations ago, and the Spanish

[2] *Man and Technology*, p. 124.

bureaucracy, who kept alive the manorial colonial system. A pure-blooded white man like Miranda and San Martín, Bolívar planned the establishment of a monarchy which was to be maintained by a purely white oligarchy. Still later, the Argentine dictator Rosas—a powerful figure in the "Prussian" style—represented and led this aristocracy against Jacobinism, which quickly spread from Mexico to the extreme south, found support in the masonic clubs antagonistic to the Church, and demanded general equality, including that of races. With that began the Indian and mestizo movement, not only against Spain, but against white blood in general: a movement which has prospered without a let-up and which today is close to its goal. Alexander von Humboldt has noted in these dominions a pride of purely Iberian origin; and even today the tradition of Basque and Visigothic lineage survives among the distinguished families of Chile. But in the prevailing anarchy since the middle of the nineteenth century the greater part of this aristocracy either succumbed or emigrated to Europe. The demagogic and warlike caudillos of the colored population dominated politics. Among them there were pure-blooded Indians of great talent, such as Juárez and Porfirio Díaz. Today the superior white race, or that which so considers itself, varies (except in Argentina) between a fourth and a tenth of the total population. In some countries, the doctors, lawyers, and even the officials are almost without exception Indians, and they have an affinity with the mestizo proletariat of the cities in their common resentment of white property holdings, whether in the hands of Creoles, Englishmen, or North Americans. In Peru, Bolivia, and Ecuador, Aymará is the second language in government and the schools. A manifest cult devotes itself to the so-called communism of the Incas, with the enthusiastic approval of Moscow. The racial ideal of a purely Indian regime is possibly quite near accomplishment.[3]

Spengler's opinions are interesting, although at times his speculations are wrong and he errs in his completely un-

[3] *Decisive Years*, p. 176.

founded judgment of the Hispano-American future. It might not be a bad idea to review certain phases of our history, focusing on it from the point of view of racial struggle. Only then could we decide, for example, whether the following judgment of Spengler is valid: "But essentially, from the revolution of Yaipin in China, the Sepoy uprising in India, and that of the Mexicans against the Emperor Maximilian, we can draw a universal conclusion: hate of the white race and a decided desire to annihilate it."

Mexico at present is vulnerable to the threat of the white man, who, if we are not careful, may overcome the country by the pacific means of financing and technology. We refer, clearly enough, to the Yankee. It is imperative that we, as men of color, take advantage of the "betrayal of technology" by assimilating modern civilization in this country—even if it is not completely compatible with our spirit—so as to avoid becoming, in the future, slaves of foreign interests. But it is just as important to benefit by the experience of other more technologically advanced countries in order to avoid a similar mechanization of our own people as they travel the road of civilization. If our native son succumbs to the vertigo of power, when he least expects it he will find himself abandoned, with an empty soul and converted into an automaton. Fortunately, we now begin to assimilate civilization in our national life at a point when other countries have run the full course of their historical evolution, and we have the necessary data for a rigorous analysis and accurate evaluation of it. We are no longer living those moments of the past century, when civilization was in its infancy and all men believed in it, when it was an idol which they worshipped unconditionally. That civilization is already growing old and the revelation of its weaknesses has so injured its reputation that man now looks upon it with great distrust. It would be an unpardonable sin if we Mexicans, in possession of all these data and able to achieve the work of civilization in full consciousness, committed the errors of other countries. Other countries can be excused because of the fact that they underwent the experience for the first time. Why then is it not possible to begin right now, by intelligent effort, a regulation of the technical growth of our country, so as to avoid an abusive mechanization of life? It is now already possible to differentiate between good and bad in the structure of civilization; with this criterion we could make use of its truly beneficial elements, escaping the calamities which other nations have suffered out of inexperience. Application of this intelligent plan would permit us, at the same time, to rescue from non-civilized life many traditional virtues, the appeal of which many Mexicans can still appreciate.

Admirable though it is, mechanical knowledge can be rationally justified only because in the future it may free man from physical labor and allow him to devote his best energy to other superior tasks in order to ennoble human nature. In Mexico we must take advantage of this initial phase in which civilization is still an unfinished process and receptive to correction. Thus we can guide our technical education in such a way that it may become a manageable instrument in man's hands. When civilization is definitively established and has a traditional structure comparable to that of old Europe, it will then be too late to attempt any sort of modification in the pattern of events. The burden of the past will be too great to admit radical changes, and man almost certainly will be fatally snared in the web of civilization, bereft of all freedom to achieve the specific purposes for which he was destined. It is true, as Goethe has said, that man is the victim of phantoms which he himself has created.

The reader may more willingly concede—as a result of these reflections—that it is now more important than ever to restore humanism to education, so as to counteract the effects of a deceitful civilization which like a modern Circe conceals the magic power of transforming men into machines, when they have fallen victim to its apparent beauty. But it is first necessary to reach beyond the conventional framework of humanistic studies—which is no more than a particular kind of discipline—and to give it the sense of a general inspiration which in our time can lift all cultural activity to a higher level.

VIII.
Education
and
Inferiority
Complex

One of the greatest concerns of national education should be the correction of certain defects of Mexican character. Character development begins at home and at school, but only in life itself is it revealed and definitively set. Nevertheless, some formative acquirements from school and family continue as nuclei, around which the traits of future personality are built. The educator can alter the influences of family and life only to a slight degree. On the other hand, school is a more flexible instrument in the teacher's hands; he is its master and can use it to carry out programs devised for specific purposes.

I have attempted to explain that some very general Mexican defects must be related to one subconscious cause: a feeling of inferiority. Actually, this sentiment cannot be interpreted as an exclusive psychic abnormality of Mexicans. Since the motives that produce it are psychological conflicts of a very universal kind, an inferiority complex appears in men of all races and nationalities. But whereas in other countries the numerous cases of that complex affect only individuals, in Mexico they have the proportions of a collective deficiency. I have already explained in this book the historical circumstances which have caused this defect, as well as the mechanism of its function. Therefore I will assume that the theory of collective deficiency has been accepted, and proceed to relate it to certain problems of Mexican education.

An inferiority complex does not appear to us as it really is. Rather, one is conscious of certain involuntary reactions which compensate for that feeling; the reactions become habits and little by little form character traits. For himself and for others, the person is simply vain, scornful, haughty, introverted, distrustful, suspicious—or otherwise. But he does not realize what these traits really mean. The manifestations of that state are therefore quite varied and often contradictory: they range from boldness, impudence, and false courage, to bashfulness or timidity. The truth is that these heterogeneous manifestations have a more-or-less visible common source: affirmation of one's own individuality at the cost of others. The same arrogant impulse moves the introvert, who scornfully remains aloof from everyone, and the man who seeks a social atmosphere in which to flaunt the virtues he lacks but would like to acquire. Self-obsession and constant attention to one's ego imply, naturally enough, a corresponding lack of interest in others, an incomprehension of the lives of one's fellow men. In brief, one's reactions to the sentiment of inferiority lead to militant individualism, which damages in varying degree one's feelings toward the community. Undeniably, the will to cooperative action and to collective discipline is weak in Mexico. In general, our life tends to dispersion and anarchy, to the obvious detriment of social solidarity. The introversion provoked by the inferiority complex logically results in a neglect of the exterior world and weakens one's sense of reality. The victim of an inferiority complex is incompatible with the world because of an incompatibility within himself, a derangement of psychic functions that unbalances his sense of judgment. He is usually the kind of person whose ambitions are out of proportion with his capabilities; his ability does not measure up to his desire. Hence the feeling of inferiority. But then it is evident that the inferiority is not real in itself but only in relation to an excessive ambition. If we restrain our desire in proportion to our ability, inferiority will have no reason for existing.

Wherever there is an inferiority complex an exorbitant thirst for power appears, for primacy in a world in which everything is seen as superior or inferior. Discord has its corollary of negative attitudes: rancor, hate, resentment, vengeance. The struggle for power in every sphere, great

and small, in private and in public, in family and in political circles, frequently leads to isolation, misanthropy,
neurosis, and so forth. All these effects disclose a resistance to community life, and it is consequently most urgent that the schools help attack the inferiority complex
from the time that it first appears in childhood.

It is not easy to set forth in detail the appropriate
methods for this purpose. This is a technical matter re-
quiring specially trained teachers who are also good psychologists. The Mexican teacher must know something
about the "cure of souls." At advanced levels he will have
to educate all over again those persons who already suffer
from maladjustment. One flaw in Mexican schools which
certainly has contributed to the preservation and even
aggravation of the inferiority complex is the lack of relationship between studies and life. In saying this I do
not mean to condone what has so often been contended:
that school should be a direct agent for the solution of
urgent practical problems. Nothing could be further from
my mind. It seems to me that education at all levels, from
elementary school to the university, should be directed
toward what I would call "knowledge of Mexico."

II

To say that our education should make the
knowledge of Mexico one of its principal aims may sound
like the repetition of a phrase once used to express hollow
patriotism or nationalism. But the truth is that we have
never really considered what this idea means, and even
less have we tried to make it effective in our schools.
Mexicans who graduate from school or from the University are notorious for knowing a great deal about other

countries and virtually nothing about their own. This constitutes a disadvantage in life, because of the frequent and immediate disparity between the individual's knowledge and the environment in which he is to live and work. Obviously, those who attend schools or the University in preparation for some technical or professional activity, do so with the intention of remaining in their own country to work. It is therefore logical to expect that their education also acquaint them with the environment that is to be their future field of action. It is the only way to forestall the avalanche of ideas, systems, and procedures from abroad which, when arbitrarily applied to Mexican problems, constitute a perilous experiment. We have already seen how such an experiment can disrupt the natural evolution of our country. The disparity between a man's circumstances and what he has learned is the origin of many failures in almost every aspect of the lives of politicians, legislators, educators, professional men, writers, and others whose education has never been attuned to practical reality. When these failures become collective they aggravate the inferiority complex. Our lack of practical sense, then, is actually a weakness in our education, which has never been realistic and which produces instead utopian and romantic men doomed to disillusion and pessimism. The example we ought to follow from more cultured countries is the only one that indeed we have not followed, i.e., education which from elementary school through college strives to inform students about their country.

Science is a universal activity which we should learn as a context of principles and methods applied to research. The knowledge of Mexico which I have stressed must be scientific, rigorous, and methodical. In the second half of the eighteenth century there was a scientific movement in Mexico, led by the disciples of Alzate. Almost all of these men were self-educated and as soon as they acquired scientific knowledge they used it to increase their knowledge of their country. They enjoyed no patronage and had to make for themselves the instruments they needed. It was they who first awakened the national consciousness. They began a distinguished tradition which deserves to be revitalized. Justo Sierra said in a memorable address that education should not create "an ideal nation of souls without a nation." True education, says the learned Sierra, should utilize every cultural source and set out "to find the means of nationalizing science, of *Mexicanizing* knowledge."

In almost all the scholastic disciplines at all levels of instruction one could make appropriate reference to national circumstances. Language and literature, especially, should be one of the bases for the foundation of national culture; then also, geography, history, the natural and biological sciences, social sciences, economics, psychology, religion, and philosophy; there is no discipline which by its principles is not in some way applicable to the knowledge of Mexico. The task of organizing an educational system of this kind is more difficult than it would seem at first. In the first place, teachers would have to be trained, and in this task the teachers colleges would perform the principal role.

The concepts of Mexico that appear in our textbooks must be revised, for they have been distorted by self-denigration and an inferiority complex. There must be enthusiasm and respect for Mexican things. Observing

our circumstances objectively, one discovers surprising
values, the knowledge of which will undoubtedly con-
tribute to uplifting the Mexican spirit. One should not
conclude that I intend to make knowledge of Mexico the
sole purpose of education; but I do believe that it is one of
the most important; and it will give the necessary substance to our national cultural programs, a substance
which up to now they have sorely lacked.

IX.
Passion
and
Interest

P assion is the note which sets the tone of
life in Mexico, especially when some private activity at-
tracts public attention. Not only politics—essentially a
public matter which here as everywhere is subject to in-
flammatory manifestations—but any event that might
excite collective interest is the immediate object of passion. Whether dealing with a scientific question or an
artistic controversy, our conversation is practically never

restrained; discussion has scarcely begun when its tone becomes exalted and electrifies the emotional atmosphere. Passion has become a basic need of our character, so that wherever there is discussion it is the inevitable way of provoking interest. Passion forces the attention seeker to exaggerate his gestures and to speak with violence in order to impress his listeners. The prestige which passion enjoys makes me doubt its truthfulness, especially in those cases where gesture and manner surpass one's intelligence.

The omnipresence of passion has made it a historical factor of first importance. Passion is the most stubborn and blind sort of motivation. When reason attempts to explain the processes which it incites, it finds them absurd, disconcerting, and empty of all logic. In a book by an English writer who visited Central America and Mexico I have read the outline of a philosophy of history, the explanatory principle of which is passion. It is Aldous Huxley's work, *Beyond the Mexique Bay*, from which I have underlined the following paragraph:

The most surprising fact about Central American wars is that none of them has had what could be interpreted as an economic cause. There has never been a question of capturing markets, destroying dangerous commercial competitors, or exploiting a province because of its valuable industrial resources. Wars in the five republics have been between conservatives and liberals, clerics and anti-clerics, those who want a federal republic and those who clamor for the sovereignty of each state. They have not been wars of interest, but of "political principles."

This idea of Huxley's interests me because it gives more importance to passion than to economic concern, contrary to the common belief that always explains things the other way around. There is no doubt that economic interest is a cause of passion, but not all passions are the result of economic interest. I refer, of course, not to individual passions but to collective passions at the point where they begin to function as historical forces. If reason is not the only force behind the social events that constitute history, there is no doubt that it always is active whenever gravely affected interests are at stake in a struggle. In every interest there is a particle of reason called calculation, which at a given moment dictates the decision to compromise in order to salvage something from a final defeat. But as far as passion is concerned, once it begins its course, it develops a blind and uncontrollable impulsiveness that knows no limits. Allain synthesizes in a perfect formula—quoted by Huxley—this essential psychological difference: "Interests can be compromised; passions will never allow compromise."

This is why one can ascribe the origin of certain historical circumstances to pure passion, without any intervention of interests in the strict sense of that term. In Hispano-American countries there are conflicts and struggles of all kinds in which calculated self-interest has no part; in the long run no one can win, and the final result is ruin for all concerned. In theory, our countries of America abound in "historical materialists," but in practice we are the most romantic race on earth. Our romanticism is immature, typical of adolescents who sacrifice reality to ideas. We are always ready to save principle, even at the cost of suicide, in obedience to that ideal which expresses the most inhuman of all attitudes: "Justice be done though the world perish."

The attentive student of history who would like to dis
cover in the maelstrom of our past some sign of continuity and coherence will find only a series of contradictions that give the impression of a chaos in which greed
contends with disinterest, and quixotry with Sancho
Panzesque materialism. Possibly this confusion comes
from applying to our own history preconceptions which
are valid only for an interpretation of European history.
I have always believed that to think of our peculiar history in a framework of foreign theories inevitably results
in complete misconception. Arguing from this point of
view one might attempt to refute our thesis as follows:
It is contended that the incentive for certain historical
acts is passion; but behind the latter lurk interests and
needs which demand satisfaction. To this I would reply
that behind these motives lurk passions which demand
satisfaction for their own sake—sacrificing altogether, if
necessary, these interests and needs. It is incomprehensible to reason, but nonetheless true, that passion annihi-
lates all, without ulterior motives. It should be clear that
I am not trying to condemn arbitrarily every impassioned attitude, for I distinguish between the passion of
interest and the interest of passion. This is no simple play
on words, but the distinction between two basic psychological realities. In one instance passion, with its impulsive power, is subservient to a vital, or even spiritual
interest. In the other, the vital or spiritual interest is subservient to passion. Passion is to be condemned, I think,
when it constitutes an end in itself, but not when it is the
means to a superior goal. What I have called the interest
of passion strives to satisfy an individual need: self-love,
vanity, pride. In a struggle of interests we may accept a

profit of fifty, or even ten, in place of one of a hundred; we say that to save something is preferable to losing all. But in a struggle of naked passions we are reluctant to permit even the most insignificant compromise of our self-love. This is axiomatic, and it explains why passions never accede to compromise. On the face of it, passion is a senseless brute force that defies all reason, but at bottom it obeys a peculiar, occult logic of its own, and with a well-determined purpose. In this last sense, passion unconsciously works toward an affirmation of the individual ego (*el yo*), to make it prevail over anyone who might oppose it. I may become impassioned over the achievement of an idea for its own sake, convinced of its ultimate virtue; or caring nothing about its value *per se*, I may seek to carry out that idea only because in that way I will seem to be right, and those who disagree with me will be humiliated.

Without intending to, I have differentiated between these two types of passion according to the psychological criteria designated by Jung as introversion and extroversion. An extrovert is a person who relates his acts, sentiments, and ideas to standards of the outside world, while the introvert recognizes no standard other than his individual ego. But in such persons not all psychic functions are categorically introverted or extroverted; in each case we need to see *what* is introverted, whether, for example, it is reason, sentiment, sensibility, or something else. As far as our problem is concerned, one may conclude that there are extroverted passions as well as introverted ones. But the point is that in all the above-mentioned types Jung has found that when the introversion is an unconscious psychic action, some other extroverted conscious action always compensates for it. It is therefore possible to show how a large number of Mexicans coincide, to some degree, with the description of these types, and how even the series of contradictions which we have pointed out are satisfactorily explained. One can tell that in the subconscious mind passion is introverted, and that in conscious thought reason is extroverted. Thus we can see that while in theory people may be positivists, materialists, or realists, in practice they act with complete disregard for reality, concerning themselves only with the affirmation of their domineering egos.

Introverted passions are a negative and destructive force in social life. They spoil the most meritorious projects, converting these into a mere pretext for their own fulfillment. For this reason so many endeavors and struggles in our history seem to make no sense, and it is depressing to see that all has been in vain. This nihilistic passion has no justification and should be fought by every possible means. Only a carefully formulated discipline will be able to change the negative sign of passion to positive. And possibly only a long and painstaking redevelopment of our education can redirect passion in such a way that it may serve a profitable objective in public life.

X.
Utopian
Youth

Mexico is one of the leading countries in opportunities available to young people. Over the past twenty years high positions in society, letters, and politics have traditionally been occupied by young people, whose spirit has prevailed in national life. In the liberal professions, in journalism, teaching, literature, and, especially, in politics, it has been possible for anyone under thirty to participate and to exercise a guiding influence in his field. Some men of my generation even believe that a man should accomplish his mission in life by his early or mid-thirties. This moment is supposed to represent the high point of achievement in life, and everything subsequent to it is considered to be relatively insignificant. I know people who feel old at thirty-five, possibly because in the physiological sense some people of that age actually are old, but in most cases it is rather that they are obsessed with the idea of age. The curious thing about this idea is that it reduces life to only two stages, and one must suddenly leap from youth to old age; no place is allowed for the crucial period of transition, which is maturity.

What is the cause of this phenomenon in Mexico, of the social and intellectual predominance of youth? Ortega y Gasset has expressed the theory that history moves in a pendular rhythm of epochs, one of old age and another of youth, which succeed each other with the regularity of a biological cycle. Without accepting this notion unconditionally—for its accuracy could be proved only by going back over the entire course of the past—I am nevertheless convinced that there has been the same kind of alternation in recent Mexican history. As I now recall its last phase, the Porfirian epoch was one of old men who, generally speaking, remained in their directive posts until about the year 1920. From this date on, when men of the Revolution everywhere began to replace men of the old regime, young people have been prominent in public life. Since that time we have seen high officials, ministers of state, for example, of less than thirty-five years of age. There is no doubt that the post-Revolutionary years in this country have been years for young people. I do not know—in the light of Ortega's theory just cited—whether the same trend has prevailed in other eras since the time of our independence. At any rate, the phenomenon is not exclusively Mexican, because it has also occurred in other countries of the world, although whether as intensely as in Mexico I do not know. Italy, Germany, Russia, and perhaps to some degree the United States, have also traditionally encouraged youth to act, at least in some fields. In most of Europe, however, the presence of certain traditional structures of life, more formal organization, and a greater density of population has made participation of young people difficult. One could say that for a European life begins at forty, especially in the field of politics. Not long ago in England a great deal of attention was given to the ascendancy to the post of Prime Minister by a man of thirty-eight, Captain Anthony Eden. It seems that he was the youngest minister in Europe.

What effects has the action of youth had in Mexican life? In its unique psychological qualities the character of youth stands out in contrast to other ages. The different stages which man goes through in his existence (childhood, youth, maturity, old age) are not, as people once thought, mere transitory phases. Rather, in some way each stage has its own purposes independent of its transitional function. Accordingly, childhood is not only a preparation for adolescence, but a phase of life which has a world of its own, with its related interests. The child's world has particular values, values in their own right, not because they lead to the aims of adulthood.

To direct child education in its entirety toward those aims is to detract from childhood. One of the principal aims that all institutions of primary education should pursue is that of having a child become a child in the fullest sense. Much the same could be said of adolescence, which also possesses its world and its particular interests. But the young person by this time can participate in the life around him and he has responsibilities which oblige him to subordinate his conduct to certain disciplines. The qualities peculiar to youth are desirable for certain activities but may turn out to be detrimental to others. Some activities, of course, belong almost exclusively to young people; for example, sports depend entirely on the young for their champions. Young people are useful in all those activities that demand energy and strength. Everyone knows that the young men are the cannon fodder of war.

Intellectual activities that require a degree of abstraction and idealism—such as poetry and philosophy— exert a powerful fascination over young people. But my purpose is not to give here a complete list of the activities which coincide with youth's way of being. My objective is rather to point out a patent circumstance in Mexican life, undoubtedly arising from youth's intervention in politics.

Politics is the most coveted objective of the will to power, simply because it is the art of achieving by power certain human aims in society. Mexicans are generally interested in politics because the will to power gives them a feeling of exaltation. But above all, a young person's interest is especially strong either because of noble idealism, or because of the exaltation and passion for politics which always lead immorally to personal profit and corruption.

The dominant tone in Mexican politics in recent years has been radicalism. Demagoguery has taken upon itself the propagation among the masses of extremist social doctrines that lack roots in Mexico, and which, given our national circumstances, are simply utopian. One could generalize by saying that political ideals have little or no relationship to the real possibilities of our country. As has been the case for the past one hundred years, we are still imitating European politics. So far very little has been done to harmonize our political trends with our natural inclinations. Our political action is usually derived by imitation from the life of other countries, and the doctrinary part we get from books. The result of this is a complete disparity between what we are and what we want to be. It is utopianism in the most precise sense. Utopianism in Mexico is due, as I see it, to a lack of feeling for reality, which is precisely one of the most characteristic psychological traits of youth. Since Mexico is a young country, our political life is affected by the youthful maladies which afflict both individual leaders and the nation as a whole.

Radicalism strives to make reality fit into an ideological scheme; but since reality has its own natural laws, such visionary pretensions are vain. It is also typical of youthful spirit to ignore reality as a value in itself and to treat it with relative indifference. The young person is interested, above all, in himself, and the surrounding world exists for him only insofar as it can give meaning to his personal feelings. All this is characteristic of an introverted mind, and introversion is one of the greatest obstacles to an objective knowledge of things. This is possibly what has weakened our faculty for objective observation and at the same time aggravated the typically fallacious notion we Mexicans have of our country. Where a poet or thinker is concerned, a degree of belief in fantasy is permissible. But it is not permissible in a politician. Politics is essentially realization; and those involved in it must be men of great practical sense, gifted with a clear understanding of the environment in which they operate. This is why utopianism is the total negation of all political sense.

I do not pretend to suggest, of course, that politics should be placed in the hands of old men, who probably would cause it to veer in a reactionary direction. I mean rather that since politics demands action on the basis of real things, it should be the work of mature men in whose mentality one finds precisely that trait lacking in young people: a sense of reality. In conclusion, if our utopian radicalism is a sign of youth, it is also one of spiritual immaturity.

XI.
The Conflict of
Generations

In recent years people in Mexico have been talking about "generations," especially in literary circles, but without defining the word, as if its meaning were obvious. Indeed, one scarcely begins to reflect on its meaning when suddenly all its vagueness and imprecision becomes apparent. Someone referring to his situation in time will say "my generation," just as formerly the common term was "my time." Of those who use the word *generation* in this way there are probably very few capable of explaining its exact meaning. As far as I know, generations were not spoken about in Mexico until people began reading Ortega y Gasset's book, *The Theme of Our Time*, in which a vital new sense is given this concept as a basis for a theory of history. This was in 1922 or 1923 and afterwards the term was used more flexibly, often excessively; generations were invented on the slightest pretext, like that phantom generation of 1915. It is worthwhile recalling what, in Ortega's view, the real scope of that idea is, as a criterion for knowing how unjustified its usage in Mexico has been.

Generation does not mean merely those of similar age who perform simultaneously in different fields of endeavor. The unity which converts a group of individuals into a "generation" comes from a mutual concept of life, even though life is expressed in many different forms and activities of culture. The same is true of art, as of thought or literature. It is quite conceivable that a group might unite because of common interest in a given enterprise, even though each of its members might have a completely different idea of life. In such cases they do not really constitute a generation. To deserve the name, a generation must be united by strong spiritual bonds, not simply by motives of expediency. It is difficult to know exactly when that ideal condition exists, because it frequently happens that a person's idea of life is insufficiently formulated: it is like the spirit submerged in the unconscious. To me it seems logical to assume that the group itself is the least capable of knowing whether or not it constitutes a generation. Only after the work is done and later evaluated in the perspective of time is it possible to tell whether the spiritual unity of the generation exists.

Ortega attributes great importance to generations, believing that they exert the motivating force behind history. As everyone knows, historical interpretation has long been disputed by two extreme theses. For some, history is moved exclusively by individuals, and the masses need only follow their will in a docile way. But what are individuals? Isolated from the mass, the individual is an abstraction. For others, the individual is nothing and the masses alone activate historical movements. They fail to see that a mass without individuals is like a body without a head and, ultimately, also an abstraction. The motivating force behind history, says Ortega, comes neither from individuals nor from the masses, but from generations. A generation is a kind of intermediate element between the mass and the individual; it is neither one nor the other, but nevertheless partakes to some extent of both. Exponents of these two distinct doctrines always find in historical events fairly convincing proof of their respective opinions. But, tested in the light of current historical reality—which, after all, is the only reality we can count on—Ortega's idea turns out to be the most accurate. Those who at present have the destiny of peoples in their hands are for better or worse the ruling minorities: it is they who govern, individuals or masses. The case of the present dictators is no proof to the contrary, for behind them is "the party" in whose name they pretend to govern, even though in possible opposition to the real will of the masses. National Socialism, Fascism, Communism are the names of political minorities in power.

A generation is therefore something much more transcendental than a mere literary group, which, to be sure, can also make history, insofar as it participates with other groups and in its own way influences the definition of an original sense of life. The value of a generation should be assessed on the basis of its work, but also on the basis of its relationship to its circumstances. Each authentic generation leaves a lasting imprint on the general culture and contributes to the formation of a national tradition. Without some continuity of generations there would be no history, which is a process of accumulation in time; it is not a series of isolated moments like movie scenes appearing in rapid and unrelated logical succession. In the latter case, life would be something that ended every evening and the next morning began again. The image of generations would be the futile struggle of Sisyphus.

There is logical continuity to the work of generations, although at times the relationship assumes a dialectical form, that is, of conflict and struggle. Generations have usually been counted in periods of fifteen years, so that four actually live simultaneously: one of children and adolescents, a second of young people, a third of mature men, and a fourth of elders. But only the two most vital generations have historical vigor, that of young people and that of mature men; since these two are the closest they are in constant dispute. In truth, worthwhile human achievements are always the work of mature men, and it is the mature generation which directs, or should direct, public affairs. In Mexico it is necessary to reiterate this platitude, because as we have previously observed, youth enters public life prematurely, and I do not know to what extent this fact is the result of overrating young people. This phenomenon has been world-wide. Everywhere the virtues of youth have been extolled. In that heightening of esteem there seemed to be at first a symptom of the vitality of our era. But responsible psychologists soon discovered that the phenomenon was simply a postwar fashion which should rather have been interpreted as a sign of fatigue and old age.

Today youth is beginning to fall out of fashion, but in the present generation it still has an exaggerated idea of its importance and rights. Young people are not entirely to blame for this attitude, because it is the natural way for youth to express itself, and an inherent defect of that age. It is typical of the juvenile mentality to consider oneself the center of the universe and the core of life. Consequently the young person would like to make a *tabula rasa* of the past and start from the beginning, like Adam in Paradise. We all have passed through this phase which, in retrospect, seems to have been mere petulance. Because of the privileged status of youth in Mexico, young people have injected some violence into the conflict of generations. Youth impulsively claims whatever it considers its right. Fortunately, the struggle is inconsequential; if it really amounted to anything, we would have in Mexico the curious case of men unable to mature, or rather, unable to use their maturity. Just as maturity would arrive ahead of time, it would also have to withdraw ahead of time, in order to accommodate the succeeding generation. The march of generations would be too quick, and they could never extract anything of value from our national culture. Collectively, the nation would not advance beyond childhood and would be unable to attune itself to the progressive civilizations of other countries. In a word, it is impossible to survive while making revolutions every day, because construction must follow destruction, and the former requires more time than the latter. It would be senseless to live only in order to destroy life, rather than to improve and enrich it. If for the sake of improvement it is sometimes necessary to undergo revolutionary chaos, one understands that the condition is a new and lasting order.

Although every recent Mexican generation has believed that it had something original to offer and has viewed the other generations with antagonism, at bottom they all have much in common. There are more similarities among their members than differences. Young people's thinking of today scarcely differs from that of 1920. If there were any significant difference there would be no common ground for dispute. In effect, the youngest fight against themselves because they confusedly sense their similarity to other generations, and they are striving to discover their own personality. Lastly, beyond individualistic passions there are obligations which must be recognized. Generations are born one after another, and according to Ortega the task of the new generation is twofold: to benefit, in the first place, by the experience of the preceding one (ideas, evaluations, etc.), and, in the second place, to exercise its own spontaneous originality. Only thus can human life travel its course without hindrance, and flow at the same time like a river, reflecting scenery that is always new.

XII.
The Use
of Thought

Thinking is not a luxury, but rather a vital necessity of man. Thought is born of life and turns to life qualities that broaden its horizons and give it depth. By virtue of thought, life is not only present but past and future as well. Thought is the possibility of making the present benefit by recollecting past experience; at the same time it is the instrument for anticipating the future. But, as far as intelligence and comprehen-

sion are concerned, thought is above all a window to the
world through which we communicate with men and
things. It is therefore our means to spiritual relationship
with society and the world, and it allows us to determine
our place in life. Thanks to knowledge, we are not lost
on our march through existence; only thus can we discover which road to travel. But the use of intelligence is,
unfortunately, neither an easy nor a secure task; it is
fraught with difficulties and constantly exposed to error.

If in the beginning, as Descartes thought, all men are
equally endowed with intelligence, it does not follow that
all know equally well how to apply it, and many are de-
prived of its benefits. One might add that some men are
reluctant to use intelligence, possibly because they have
not been taught its potentialities, or because their temperament restrains them. We should remember that intelligence does not have equal preponderance over other
psychic forces (such as will and sentiment) in every race.
In some races will is the guiding force in life; in others,
sentiment; in still others, intelligence or reason. All have
heard the well-known opinion that the Hispanic race to
which we belong has not distinguished itself in history
by the products of its thought; by implication, then, it is
an unintelligent race. But the truth is that a quite different spiritual force has assumed the direction of life: sentiment, or more precisely, passion. Intelligence is there, but
subordinated, enslaved by other more potent drives which
infringe upon it and impede its movements. This, at least,
seems to be the case with Mexicans. The contact I have
had with a large number of young people at the University convinces me that our race is well endowed with intelligence. The young Mexican who has not yet suffered

the mental deformations that life produces can make intelligence work freely, and just as well, I believe, as that of any of the "superior" races.

The work of some thinkers and scientists shows, moreover, that our intelligence is not inferior to that of the Europeans. But if this fact is to constitute the rule rather than the exception, there will have to be a change in circumstances, which today are scarcely conducive to intellectual activity. Young countries must first organize and develop their material existence in order to attend later to less pressing needs. Deep meditation and abstract thought are fruits of a liberation which is possible only when the elementary problems of life have been solved.

This does not mean that one can actually live without thinking. Only at the cost of lowering life to the most abject level would such an existence be possible. Without thought, man would vegetate in the obscurity of instinct and scarcely surpass the level of animal existence. In justice to our race we should recognize that ideas have played a role of considerable importance in our history, to the extent that if criticism is deserved it is due to the frequent preference of ideas to everything else. Utopianism is no more than an exaggerated rationalism, or the innocent assumption that reality submits to the dictates of reason.

If in Mexico, then, there exists some capacity for thought, it has yet to be effectively developed and disciplined. The primary cause of the exercise and development of intelligence is the urge to know the truth about all that is problematical in life. It is not easy to submit oneself continuously to truth, because truth is not always pleasant, nor does it answer to the most intimate demands of the will. There are accordingly many individuals who deceive themselves, declaring to be true that which they would like to be true. Dignified exercise of the intelligence requires effort, sometimes painful, and intellectual and moral discipline. The thinking person must protect not only his learning process, but also his entire spirit, against the many subjective influences that will result from his inquiries. No one ignores the fact that this self-criticism is extremely difficult to practice. That is why veracity is considered a virtue of great worth. Are there many truthful people in Mexico? I should like the reader to answer this question for himself, relying on his own experience and discretion.

I limit myself to pointing out how readily ideas and theories imported from Europe are accepted in Mexico without any criticism whatsoever; this betrays a minimal effort and idleness of spirit. I wonder if our tendency to imitate, especially in philosophy, is not really idleness in disguise. Aside from all these circumstances that weaken thought, one cannot ignore the fact that truth has not, by any means, been indispensable to our social and political existence. Our national life is ensnared in a thick web of deceptive appearances and conventional lies which are deemed essential to its sustenance. Truth is relegated to the category of an undesirable object.

In spite of all this I still believe that the cultivation of thought and reflection in every activity is an urgent necessity in Mexico. It seems to me that many abortive projects, many errors and deviations, are due not to evil intent but to a lack of reflection, to an insufficient and inadequate use of intelligence. I do not mean to say that talent is lacking; there is simply an erroneous application of it.

If in using our talent we fail to be objective and to direct it toward precise objectives, its efficiency will be nullified.

For some time I have wanted to show that the only legitimate course in Mexico is to think as Mexicans. This must seem like a trivial and platitudinous affirmation; but in our country it is a necessary one, because we often talk as if we were foreigners, far removed from our spiritual and physical surroundings. All thought must be based on the assumption that we are Mexicans and have to see the world in our own perspective, as the logical consequence of our geographic destiny. It naturally follows that the object or objects of our thought should be those right around us. Seeking knowledge in the world at large, we shall have to see it through the particular circumstance of our little Mexican world. It would be a mistake to interpret these ideas as the mere result of narrow-minded nationalism. It is rather a question of ideas which have a philosophical motivation. Only the man who can see the world about him in his own perspective has vital thought. Leibnitz said that every individual reflects the world in his own way. This, however, does not mean that there are many truths, but one only. It is logical to suppose that concerning any one object no more than one truth can exist, for if there are many, none is *truth*. A spherical segment seen from one side is concave, from the other, convex. Therefore, two individuals who see this object from opposite points will have two different views of it; each will be partial, but within this limitation they will each see the truth.

By disciplined action, Mexico needs to cultivate an authentic style of national thought, and its truth or context of truths, just as other countries have done. As long as this is missing we will be vulnerable to strange ideas which, having nothing to do with our needs, will eventually deform our national character and create problems still more serious than those now at hand. I believe that all men in our country who can think must take the responsibility for withdrawing—though it be only momentarily—from the whirlwind of life, so as to explore objectively the various realms of Mexican reality. Great regions of this reality are entirely unknown; they have not yet been formulated in concepts. It seems to me that the tasks awaiting our consideration are essentially two: 1) What is each aspect of Mexican existence really like? 2) What should it be like, within the limits of possibility? The most concrete and detailed definition of problems to be solved, that is, the statement of Mexican problems, is a preliminary theme, and perhaps the most difficult one to study. We'll postpone for a while our attempt to define in precise formulas any of the basic problems of Mexico.

XIII.
Pedantry

Pedantry undoubtedly has its own end, although its purpose is often difficult to recognize. It is not inconceivable that the pedant himself *may* be unware of this purpose. Every pedant gives the impression of being and actor in a play, and pedantry is a mask which conceals or disguises something. What is it that pedantry tries to hide?

First, pedantry and the pedant must be defined. Pedantry is a form of expression ascribed almost exclusively to the intellectual, or whoever appears to be one. It is especially common among professors, literati, artists, and writers of all kinds, and is expressed in spoken or written language. In a man's everyday conduct pretension or vanity are to be expected, but not pedantry. Pedantry is a style of speaking or writing, an unmistakable intonation of the voice. The pedant uses an affected style, although not all affectation in language is pedantic. It is so only when the language reveals the author's intention to pride himself on his talent, wisdom, or erudition. The pedant seizes every occasion to exhibit before audiences great and small his prodigious qualities. To be sure, one characteristic of authentic pedantry is inopportuneness; its most conspicious exponents are precisely those who are always overbearing, who set up professorial chairs wherever they are. We hear them speaking of profound things in the midst of a familiar conversation, flouting famous names or celebrated quotations in the least appropriate circumstances. In a word, the pedant is always disliked because of his tactlessness and indiscretion. In every social relationship he sounds a discordant note in his strange tone and language. As for social behavior, there is no doubt that the pedant belongs to a well-peopled species of misfits. This observation is possibly a good clue to the secret of pedantry.

The pedantic gesture is an obvious attempt to assert one's superiority, but in an aggressive and scornful way. The pedant seems to say, "I am the only one here who's worth anything; the rest of you are imbeciles." But he deceives no one, and others see through the falsity of his pretensions. Far from achieving recognition and admiration, the pedant awakens only antipathy and repugnance.

He turns out to be an entirely unsociable person. In general, pedants are rabid individualists, incapable of understanding anyone else's qualities and unwilling to take part in any cooperative effort. Occasionally, however, he does attract groups of innocent or ignorant admirers who are awe-struck by his words. The tragic thing is that pedantry always requires an audience, just as a theater requires spectators. The pedant does not simply want to attract attention and to be heard; he also seeks the approval and applause of the little world around him.

If we were to classify pedantry as a more general vice, we could not find a better category than vanity; pedantry is one of the multiple facets of this vice, against which no human being dares to cast the first stone.

Generally speaking, the common meaning of words contains a clear insight into the heart of the things they identify. In the dictionary we find that the word *pedant* was used to designate a "teacher of grammar who teaches children in their homes." Then, "With reference to one who because of ridiculous conceit, takes pleasure in making untimely and vain boasts of erudition which he may or may not have." Pedantry is defined as "a fondness for the airs and ways of a learned person. The urge to appear superior to others and to teach them." Thus, the original connotation of words determines with complete accuracy the characteristics of this curious type of expression. Undoubtedly, pedantry has a scholastic origin. Pedants swarm among the teachers and students in the universities, seeking fame for their wisdom. Academic circles address the outside world in order to reach the cultured class. Their preference has always been for professional and intellectual groups.

But what is the psychological mechanism of pedantry? I have already said that the pedant is a misfit, and his inadaptability consists of a desire for intellectual superiority out of proportion to his real talent or knowledge. The disproportion between his ambition and what he actually is provokes his conscience to a painful conflict that results in an inferiority complex. When the desire to achieve the highest position is so imperative that it will make no compromise with reality, fiction is the only source of satisfaction. The individual converts his life into a comedy of superiority, deceiving himself in a role in which he can temporarily restore equilibrium to a mind harassed by an inferiority complex. Pedantry is therefore neither more nor less than a disguise, a mask which the person uses to conceal a weakness; that weakness is his intellectual poverty. But the success of this ruse depends on his being the first to believe in his own words and to interpret the comedy convincingly. At the beginning of this chapter we ventured to say that pedantry has a purpose which is difficult to recognize, and now we can confirm this. If the pedant tries to achieve in those around him a favorable opinion regarding his worth, he does so only as a means of self-persuasion and of recovering confidence in himself. The important thing is to cover up the spiritual void that depresses him and diminishes his worth in his own eyes. Unfortunately, the comedy is awkward, and the spectators are malicious. Ultimately the pedant is forced to content himself with distinction in circles that are modest and easy to please, and in which success gains neither merit nor satisfaction.

APPENDIX I

*Justo Sierra and the Political
Evolution of Mexico*

Recent publication of the *Political Evolution of Mexico* by the Casa de España has made available a great historical work which is destined to become a classic. This edition may rightfully be considered the first, because the preceding ones were difficult to obtain and one often had the impression that Justo Sierra's work had remained unpublished for many years. It was high time that a history of quality was made accessible to the reading public.

More than any other kind of work, a national history is vulnerable to the impassioned criticism and the preconceived notions of average readers, especially when they have not lived in the author's time or even in the time of scholars who can object in detail to any given point on the basis of new research. For history there are no definitive or absolute truths; it is a science open to constant revision. It is therefore reasonable to suppose that the work of Justo Sierra is subject, like any other of its genre, to a reinterpretation of many details. But in this case we are not concerned with details, even though Sierra was an honest and scrupulous historian who never accepted anything unconfirmed by authorized sources. The value of his work is in its historical vision as a whole, and in its admirable synthesis of the evolution of the Mexican people. Until another historical synthesis is written, strengthened by the data of new research, Sierra's book will continue to excel as the high point of Mexican historical science.

The *Political Evolution of Mexico* is a great history because it is not the work of a specialist. Justo Sierra was not a professional historian devoted to examining archives or to unearthing archeological objects. He had a great mind and a universal vision of things; that is, in his thinking he was a philosopher. But in his sensibility he was a poet, and both these qualities of his temperament coincided in a vocation which required both, in unison. Therefore, Justo Sierra chose the highest of historical missions, that which the specialist cannot accomplish, because he can't see the forest for the trees and he lacks the imagination to give life and color to facts which he knows only in fossilized form. Justo Sierra achieved what every age should achieve with the raw material of past events: he molded it into a meaningful synthesis, which in effect is the only way of making history culturally significant.

One of the rare merits of this historical vision is a sense of proportion which does honor to the name of its author. Usually Mexican historians have failed to interpret events accurately: sometimes because an inferiority complex led them to minimize their significance; at other times because, through narrow-mindedness or ignorance of universal history, the magnification of events or personages has given our history mythological importance, as an elementary school child might see it. Only a mind like Justo Sierra's can see Mexican history as part of universal history, giving the correct sense of proportion to each element and its due place in the scale of human evolution. This hierarchal sense of importance and value makes things appear as they really are, without exaggerating or diminishing them; it is objectivity in the finest sense. Objective vision is the historian's maximum virtue, his quality *sine qua non*. Historical truth is conditioned by what a people may or may not do. If that truth lives in Justo Sierra's writings, it is because he had a profound knowledge of the Mexican people, and their capacities and limitations. It is because he could discern in past events what was possible and what was not. Neither his love nor his sterling patriotism could distort reality in his mind, bitter as reality was at times. He understands and forgives all that history reveals of human weakness, but he does not attempt to conceal it. The reader of Sierra's history will discover all the essential characteristics of the Mexican people, their qualities and defects. Their drama, which is sometimes depressing and painful, has found humane and benevolent judgment and the necessary understanding.

Any just evaluation of the effort represented by Sierra's history should take into account the difficulties the author had to overcome at a moment of national life when previous research in historical science was scarce and totally confused. Justo Sierra believed that he was undertaking a task beyond his capability. In his book he refers to the problem as follows:

My apprehension was to be expected in a country in which statistical projects are scarcely getting under way. There has been but inadequate and isolated appreciation of collected and classified data; our libraries—still disorganized, without cata-

logues or facilities for consultation—are immense stacks of
old papers which time and negligence have nearly reduced to
dust; and our writers have inevitably made partisan weapons
of their works, basing their valuation only on the most apparent and hastily established facts, and combining the theories they have used to interpret our history with the prejudices that have falsified it.

Like the work of so many others in Mexico and America,
Justo Sierra's is the result of a successful individual effort to overcome the limitations of circumstances by
sheer intelligence.

Justo Sierra is fully aware of the scientific character
of history, and as a historian, he interprets the significance of events from the standpoint of the predominant
ideas of his time. His mind was trained and developed in
the atmosphere of positivism which characterizes the
whole Porfirian era. He sums up the doctrine by which
he has interpreted history in these words: "Society is a
living organism; accordingly, it grows, develops, and
changes. This perpetual transformation quickens in close
relation to the inner energy of the social organism, by
means of which it combats external elements in order to
assimilate them and make them aid its progress." Justo
Sierra adopts ideas from the positivist sociology of Comte,
Littré, and Spencer in order to explain our history. For
example, he believes that during the Porfirian epoch
transition from the military phase to the industrial phase
was taking place, just as Spencer theorizes in his *Sociology*. Recognizing all the lapses in our history and its
present and future perils, he views Mexican social evolution with all the optimism of the progressive philosophy which was foisted upon us by positivism. But this
does not mean that Justo Sierra suffered the limitations
of a partisan or academic thinker. His spirit had a full-

ness, a vigor, and a drive that could not be held to the narrow limits of an "ism." His assimilation of all the great ideas of European culture made him into one of the most eminent personalities in Hispano-America. His stature is comparable to that of the great humanists of the Renaissance. The admirable thing about this man who scaled the spiritual heights of America is his great faith in Mexico, his great love for his native land. We might say that the history he wrote with such honesty and objectivity was only a means of awakening Mexicans to patriotism. Such is the meaning of this passage, in which the historian accedes to the educator:

To give the native son social dignity (only because of our apathy does he lack it) and make him the master of a richly cultivated land; to identfy his spirit and ours by the unifying elements of language, aspirations of love and hate, mental and moral criteria; to excite in him the divine ideal of a nation for all, of a great and happy nation; to create, finally, the national soul: this is the goal assigned to future endeavor; this is the program of national education. Everything that aspires to its realization, and only that, is patriotic. Every obstacle which tends to hold it back or lead it astray is meanness, betrayal— our enemy.

The models who inspired Justo Sierra in spirit and form were the liberal and positivist French historians such as Guizot (initiator of liberal interpretation in history), Michelet, Taine, and Renan. Justo Sierra thinks of historical evolution as a great progressive movement that leads to the achievement of freedom. Freedom in the broadest sense is the ideal to which the Mexican people should aspire as the final goal of their social evolution. However, Sierra's historical thinking, in its application to Mexico, extends beyond his time and opens up many far-sighted perspectives. Little or nothing would have to be changed in his book in order to bring it up to date; this proves that it is written from a point of view superior to a partisan political attitude which might have distorted its historical authenticity. As a writer he vitalizes his scientific work with one of the finest prose styles in Hispano-America. The result of this high quality in content and form makes Justo Sierra the insuperable master of Mexican history.

APPENDIX II

Concerning Mexican Character

The recent abundance of studies about the Mexican is not simply the result of a caprice or quirk of thought, nor the work of improvisation. It is the symptom of a restless conscience provoked by both external and internal causes. The external causes can be seen in the crisis of the Revolution of 1910 and in a world historical situation conducive to an analysis of regional life. The internal causes, however, are embodied in the maturing of the Mexican spirit, which in coming of age has experienced the growth of its own individuality. Interest in things Mexican could not have come from a void, or from the mere desire to seek out something which does not exist. If the restlessness has become general it is because the nucleus of that individuality already existed, not as a finished entity, but as a living process. On the other hand, I can see that our enthusiasm for self-knowledge is animated by the conviction that it is the most urgent and appropriate task for thinkers of our day. To parody the famous saying of Pope, the proper study of the Mexican is the Mexican. Eighteen years ago I introduced a doctrine which was a variation on this theme, in a well-known essay which had great resonance, if only the resonance of a solitary voice.[1] From the beginning I was aware that the theme was of such magnitude that it exceeded the capacities of one man. Today I witness the realization of a hope I had never lost: that the theme would interest a number of educated men who would attack the problem from different angles and enrich knowledge about the Mexican through a rigorous examination of the varied expressions of his life. Only a collective contribution can give results appreciable enough to affect decisively the direction of our life and culture. I would be the first, therefore, to praise and encourage all who have seriously devoted their intellectual energy to this theme, whatever might be their point of emphasis and method. I believe it is the theme which deserves priority among the philosophical, historical, and anthropological disciplines of Mexico, for on it depends the most genuine expression of our national life and culture. Recent studies have suggested many thoughts to me, some simply clarifying my own ideas, which in my judgment can be useful in defining some of the fundamental points of the question. Many people have asked whether I have continued my reflections on the Mexican and his culture, and have even urged me to continue them. I should now like to reply by saying that if up to now I have not continued, the delay may be due to a peculiar condition of my mental mechanism, which does not act except by way of reaction: that is, after my ideas have stimulated the growth of other ideas of opposite or of simply different nature. This means

[1] Ramos refers, of course, to the first edition of *Profile of Man and Culture in Mexico*, published in 1934. (Translator's note)

that my thought about the Mexican remained static over the years in which no one concerned himself with the problem. Therefore, this unforeseen and very rich harvest of ideas on Mexican life was necessary for a renewal of my own reflections.

One question about the characterization of the Mexican is the following: To what kind of Mexican do these traits belong? Are they equally applicable to whites and Indians? Notwithstanding racial diversity, the differences are not, in my judgment, as profound as they seem. The mestizos and Creoles have much in common with the Indian. Even though the Spanish conquerors dominated the Indians by their superiority in civilization, the fact remains that in another sense they were themselves conquered. Since the sixteenth century, as L. González y G. has shown, the Spaniards were influenced by the language, customs, and atmosphere of indigenous life, to the extent that one can speak about mixture of culture as well as of blood. In our time the Indian continues to mix in the economic, cultural, and political life of the nation. He participates in it agriculturally, industrially, and spiritually; his folklore permeates the arts; and when he leaves his community to join city life, he demonstrates his aptitudes by competing, in equal circumstances, in business, politics, and the intellectual professions. His differences from whites and mestizos are generally those of social and economic condition. This causes a disadvantage on the cultural level, but it implies no mental inferiority. Considered in its entirety, the indigenous environment is the true background, the "hinterland," of Mexican culture.

Another obstacle to treating the Mexican as a general type is the existence of regional groups in distinct geographical and climatic zones of the nation. The inhabitants can be classified as follows: those of the high plateau comprising the cool central region of the country; those of the tropical and coastal areas; and finally the northerners and the Yucatecans. But these differences do not actually affect national unity. Even though the groups are separated by great distances, revolutionary repercussions have tended to mobilize them and to induce them to communicate with each other. Especially the last Revolution, which displaced them in every sense, resulted in a complete intermingling of all the country's inhabitants —northerner and southerner, westerner and easterner, underdog and opportunist. All were mixed and thrown together as if the country were an immense cocktail shaker. More recently, progress and modernization in communications has cut distances and facilitated travel, thereby enabling Mexicans of different regions to become better acquainted. It should be emphasized that regional distinctions persist in all countries, even in the old European nations where national unity is indisputable. Take, for example, Spain. Andalusians, Castilians, Basques, Galicians, Catalans, and so forth, are all of the universal Spanish type, even though such profound differences as language exist among them. In this regard there is greater difference between an Andalusian and a Catalan than between a Yucatecan and a northerner. Let us remember that England is a united kingdom joining the Scotch, Irish, English and other peoples. Italy and Germany show the same heterogeneity. In every state of the Mexican Republic Spanish is spoken by all except a native minority, which has preserved its native tongue. The Virgin of Guadalupe is venerated everywhere; everywhere the same songs are sung; and bullfights are enthusiastically received in every town. Our regional distinctions are probably less noticeable than those of a number of European countries, but they are enough to give color to our nation as a whole.

Some years ago I took the liberty of pointing out certain characteristics peculiar to the Mexican. In similar ways others have added to his profile. But one often tends to forget that these studies have been made in the spirit of nationalism inherent in the word "Mexican." There has even been doubt as to whether political ideas of national structure should be taken into account. It must be emphasized, in other words, that nationality in the politically abstract or legalistic sense does not influence individual character. In this specific instance we are thinking of nationality in a more vital, concrete sense: in a context of collective experiences—past and present—which are the result of collective undertakings. The concept includes socially active individuals' recollection of achievement and failure, misfortune and joy. The sum of living experiences and the memory of times past are present in every human being in a region of the psyche called "collective consciousness." The ego stems from this consciousness and is permanently dependent on it. Thus the gregarious character of man is a variable force, but always a factor in the development of his individual conduct. Now these collective experiences motivate a value judgment regarding nationality which is not always objective or fair because of intervening emotions. Strong as the grass-roots feeling may be in national sentiment, there is always a compensating valuation which in some instances results in the extreme of complete alienation from the native earth. Legitimately or not, this conception of nationality becomes an element of collective thought, and eventually one of many prejudices affecting the conduct of individuals. At this stage of development nationalism is extremely dangerous, for its effects persist even after their true motivation has disappeared. Nationalism gives rise to strong emotional reactions, as everyone knows, and is one of the mainsprings of private and public behavior.

Outstanding events of our nineteenth-century history led to the formulation of Mexican nationality, events which constituted a series of quite adverse collective experiences. When independence had been achieved, Mexicans found themselves unprepared for political life; a period of disorder began in which the nation constantly tottered between anarchy and dictatorship. Thus weakened, Mexico was no match for the United States in the War of 1847 and in defeat lost a significant portion of her territory. The unbalance continued with the ceaseless struggles among political parties, making inevitable the instability of all institutions. Maximilian's empire and French intervention were a further blow to national autonomy. Frequent civil wars weakened the economy and aggravated general impoverishment. The Porfirian regime[2] favored only the ruling class; public education was in a precarious state and higher education was scarce. It was quite natural, then, that these misfortunes should lead to "self-denigration," that is, to a negative view of nationality. A factor not to be ignored is foreign opinion, which is usually magnified or exaggerated in its view of Mexico as a backward country, continuously wallowing in chaos and incivility. From the campaign of disrepute commonly associated with Poinsett,[3] to the North

[2] I.e., the regime of Porfirio Díaz, president and dictator from 1877 to 1910. (Translator's note)

[3] Joel R. Poinsett (1779–1851) was U.S. Minister to Mexico from 1825 to 1829. During this time he arranged to have charters sent from the Masons' Grand Lodge of New York to incipient Freemason groups in Mexico. His report on a previous visit, *Notes on Mexico, Made in 1882: with an Historical Sketch of the Revolution*, was published in 1824. In the

American news services' worldwide circulation of accounts of the Revolution of 1910, Mexico was inundated by unfavorable opinions that added to a general lowering of national esteem by Mexicans themselves. One result of this devaluation was a mutual distrust among Mexicans; another was a weakening of the social spirit of solidarity and cooperation. Men now felt more strongly the need to rely on their individual resources.

A defensive instinct tends to expel from the conscience all painful and depressing feelings. Accordingly, the national inferiority complex is submerged in subconsciousness, and individuals do what they can to form a favorable idea of themselves, which—though illusory—is taken as authentic, and it serves as compensation for depressing ideas. With the beginnings of independent life also comes the beginning of this intimate process in the Mexican spirit which expresses itself in the intent to dissimulate, cover up, or falsify reality through the imitation of European models. In a way, this attitude coincides with the kind of utopianism that aspires to submit reality to theories or formulae which are judged infallible because of their successful application in other places and circumstances. Utopianism took the place of reality and experience, and forgotten was the rudimentary truth that ideas are successful only when they come from immediate, circumstantial experience.

This exposition has attempted to show why any study of Mexican character must refer to individuals primarily as members of the national community. Whoever explores the theme of character will have to take into ac-

---

1840's he became an outspoken opponent of war against Mexico. However, Poinsett's anti-Catholicism, his militant liberalism, and his intolerance of certain aspects of Mexican social and political life earned him a generally poor reputation in Mexican histories. (Translator's note)

count the history of our nationality, for man insofar as he possesses national characteristics is the product of history. Nationality is more than a political category; it is also an existential trait of the persons who make up that category. Thus, in asking for a definition of the Mexican, we are actually inquiring into his consciousness of nationality, in an effort to discover how such a consciousness has influenced his being and behavior.

Social creature that he is, man cannot rely exclusively on his own resources to sustain himself. The individual's life is made possible only by the establishment of that local and national relationship which can give him his environment and means of subsistence, ranging from language to specific material necessities. Life in common creates in each person a feeling of solidarity which in turn gives strength and inspiration to personal action. Insignificant as he may be as an individual, the citizen of a powerful nation conducts himself abroad with confidence and tact, because he can rely on the backing of his nationality. In affirming that the Mexican suffers an inferiority complex, I have always meant that this complex affects his *collective* consciousness. If the sense of nationality is undermined by a feeling of inferiority, there is likely to be a pronounced impulsive reaction. In normal situations individualistic tendencies are counterbalanced by the moderating action of collective sentiments. But there can be no normality when this counterbalance is lacking and individualism asserts itself uncontrolled. This very unbalance explains a great number of Mexican character traits, many of which are different and even contradictory. But the common denominator for all of them is their antisocial nature, including distrust, aggressiveness, resentment, timidity, haughtiness, deception, and so on.

I am quite aware that these chacteristics were present in Mexicans of the colonial era, who for different reasons developed a similar personality. Social life of that time abounded in injustices which left the Creole at a disadvantage in relation to the peninsular Spaniard, who was always a recent arrival. In his lowly condition the mestizo was worse off still. Because of his inability to get what he wanted he cultivated a kind of reticence in order to cover up his thoughts, and his language had a propensity to falsehood and euphemism. What information we have about Mexicans of the colonial period points up the similarity between their conduct and our own. Quite possibly there were changes for the better in the late eighteenth century, but in the agitated atmosphere of the past century, and for reasons we have already set forth, old attitudes returned. However, in explaining the development of that conduct we showed that it has always been abnormal and misleading, a disguise with which the Mexican has endeavored to conceal his true character. Other investigators have accepted and reaffirmed this point of view; Octavio Paz, for example, calls the Mexican's conduct a mask. Behind this mask he discovers an inclination to solitude which the title of his book expresses, *The Labyrinth of Solitude*.[4] But a more realistic observation would show, contrary to Paz's thesis, that solitude is not the result of voluntary choice, but rather of a disrupting element that makes human character antisocial. Solitude is only a refuge which is sought unconsciously. The Mexican does not desire or enjoy solitude. Rather, solitude afflicts him because of his timidity, his touchiness, and his distrust—all of which are clothed in inhibitions. The love or taste for solitude is the exclusive

---

[4] *El laberinto de la soledad*, Fondo de Cultura Económica, México, 1959.

asset of men endowed with an intense and rich inner life, and only in solitude itself can solitude become a joy. It constitutes an aristocracy of the spirit, the exceptional possession of poets, philosophers, or mystics. It is not culti-vated by the common man.

The Mexican Revolution was, among other things, a nationalistic movement. It uncovered a false Mexico, imi-tative of Europe and led by the Frenchified regime of Porfirianism. It vindicated the Indians by reinstating them in the national community. It is true that before the Revolution was over, the return to native values was corrupted by a false nationalism symbolized in the Mex-ican horseman and festive dresses *à la china poblana*. But the Revolution was nevertheless the moment when the main cause of national failure was recognized as the in-discriminate substitution of foreign remedies for a quest of solutions naturally adaptable to the problems them-selves. Finally the absurd desire to imitate was cured. It was then that Mexicans realized they had lived in ignor-ance of their own reality, and now they felt the urgency to observe and comprehend it. For the first time new eco-nomic, social, and political systems were seriously con-sidered, including those without a foreign trademark.

Signs of the new nationalism soon appeared in culture and education, which had also suffered from European imitation. The revolutionary crisis led to a rediscovery of Mexico by penetrating the false appearances which had obscured her true nature. Thus for the first time the question of self-knowledge was dealt with in precise terms, and the way is now clear for a direct approach to Mexican reality. Such is the present state of studies on Mexican culture.

I dare say that this year's series of lectures in the School

of Philosophy and Letters will constitute a memorable
event in the history of our culture, and will help rectify
the erroneous tendency of Mexicans to ignore rather than
to examine and evaluate the basic reality of their lives.[5]
The fact that a large number of scholars—especially
young scholars—have devoted thought to this problem
shows that it is being appraised anew. Its importance as
the basis of our existence, i.e., of the originality of our existence, has been recognized. Since I happen to have begun this type of interpretation only a few years ago,
scholars today often refer to my ideas. Among these ref-
erences is one in the valuable essay by Emilio Uranga,
who in discussing my idea of the Mexican's inferiority
complex, proposes that the concept "inferiority" be re-
placed by that of "inadequacy."[6] In the distinction he
makes between the concepts of inferiority and inadequacy, he accurately states that inadequacy implies an
inherent sense of values. The feeling of inadequacy includes recognition of a hierarchy of values, whereas inferiority is the result of a subterfuge against that hierarchy. I am in complete agreement with Uranga's
analysis but wonder if any valid characterization could
allow substitution of the term inadequacy for that of
inferiority. Does the average Mexican have an inherent
sense of values? Does he recognize a hierarchy of values?

[5] Ramos refers to lectures of the series "The Mexican in Search of the
Mexican" (*El mexicano en busca del mexicano*) given at the National
University of Mexico in January and February, 1951. Three of these, in-
cluding Ramos' own (which appears here as this Appendix), were pub-
lished in *Cuadernos Americanos*, X (mayo-junio, 1951), No. 3, 87–128.
The other two were "Dialéctica de la conciencia en México" by Leopoldo
Zea (pp. 87–103), and "Notas para un estudio del mexicano" by Emilio
Uranga (pp. 114–128). (Translator's note)

[6] See Emilio Uranga (Note 5), *loc. cit.*, pp. 120–122.

I have already said that the Mexican "is extraordinarily sensitive to criticism, and he holds it at bay, ever ready to thrust abusive language at his fellow man. For this reason, self-criticism remains paralyzed. He needs to convince himself that others are inferior. He therefore admits no superiority and is ignorant of the meaning of veneration, respect, and discipline. He is ingenious in detracting from others to the point of annihilating them." (above, p. 71) In several passages of this book I have referred to the Mexican's rejection of values. To prove my assertion I need resort to no other evidence than general consensus. If the reader quickly recollects his experiences and his personal observations he will certainly confirm what I have said. Intellectuals, as well as people of average culture, reveal every day the injustice of their appraisals. Only in exceptional cases do I believe the Mexican possesses that virtue of triple veneration which Goethe defined as every man's need: veneration for what is above him, beside him, and below him. If the trait we have observed in many Mexicans tends to disrupt their sense of values, one must conclude in the light of Uranga's reasoning that Mexicans suffer an inferiority complex, and not one of inadequacy. I have sometimes wondered whether Uranga himself unconsciously thinks as he does in order to free himself from this same inferiority complex. His essay is an eloquent plea for all Mexicans to cure themselves of their inferiority complex by recognizing that it is actually only a question of inadequacy. In this sense I applaud his idea, especially since my own book recommends the same approach; the Mexican must measure his life by his own criteria and cease comparing it to lives measured by other standards. But if the main question is to know not what the Mexican should be but what he actually is, I believe my conclusion is the more valid. Ultimately there appears to be in Uranga some confusion between the real and the ideal Mexican.

Uranga states that the study of the Mexican should be ontological, and that my essay tends in that direction without reaching its goal. But my essay is not ontological, for the simple reason that I did not intend it to be. It was my more modest intention to acquire a knowledge of the Mexican, or an *autognosis* as José Gaos has put it. To argue about whether a study of the Mexican should be ontological or not seems somewhat idle, since such a question depends on intentions and possibilities. The real question is one of goals—any one of which may be possible, but all of which are different. Nothing need impede anyone from setting out to write an ontology of the Mexican. But whoever does so assumes a responsibility he is obliged to fulfill, provided, of course, that the ontology be conceived in conformity with the Mexican, and not that the Mexican be conceived in conformity with some ready-made ontology, simply to give credence to the latter. Theoretical speculation is not only permissible but an indispensable instrument for study of the Mexican. Theory, however, should be limited at all times to its instrumental function; it ought not—as a means—to usurp attention from the proposed end, which is knowledge about the Mexican. This, then, brings us to a consideration of the danger to which the investigator is always susceptible; for indeed one thing is to use a philosophy in order to explain the Mexican, another is to use the Mexican in order to explain a philosophy. In the first case we can be reasonably sure that the philosophical instrument will help us discover the truth about the Mexican of flesh and blood. In the second case we are deluded into thinking we have found in the Mexican what had previously been concluded in the philosophy.

It seems to me that too much emphasis has been placed on abnormal aspects of Mexican character, which, to be sure, are at first sight the most impressive. It is true that an interpretation of these anomalies has constituted an essential phase in the analysis of the fictitious elements of our national character. But I think the time has come to consider the more normal manifestations, as it were, of Mexican life. In these the foundation of our being can truly be seen. Based only on an analysis of anomalies, the profile would be unilateral and incomplete, and, consequently, false. The only legitimate premise for our interpretation—or any interpretation of a similar nature—is concrete reality. Whatever form the reality may assume—historical events, social behavior, this or that type of personality, works of art—we cannot afford to lose contact with it. In my book, which others have quoted so freely, I state that the greatest human achievements in Mexico are cultural, the product of what I call "creole culture." I say that "from this *humus* of generic culture has grown a kind of selectivity, also creole, that has shown itself in a small number of personalities. . . . Due to their quality as *men* they have reached the highest level to which a Hispanic American can aspire." (above, p. 76)

And now I add that in personalities such as these it is possible to find the true Mexican. It is they who possess a legitimate superiority, they who are less susceptible to deceit and evasiveness than those other Mexicans who have distorted their basic nature. They are men whose natural superiority leaves no room for an inferiority complex.

A BIBLIOGRAPHY OF SAMUEL RAMOS

I. Books and Monographs

Hipótesis, 1924–1927, Ediciones Ulises, México, 1928.

El caso Strawinsky, Ediciones de la Revista Contemporáneos, México, 1929.

El perfil del hombre y la cultura en México, Imprenta Mundial, México, 1934, 179 pp.; 2nd edition, Editorial Pedro Robredo, 1938, 182 pp.; 3rd edition, Espasa-Calpe (Colección Austral, No. 1080), Buenos Aires-México, 1951, 145 pp. *Diego Rivera*, Imprenta Mundial, México, 1935; 2nd edition, Universidad Nacional Autónoma de México, Dirección General de Publicaciones (Colección de Arte, No. 4), 1958, 200 pp.

Más allá de la moral de Kant. A. Chapero (Cuadernos de México Nuevo, No. 5), 1938, 39 pp.

Hacia un nuevo humanismo: Programa de una antropología filosófica, La Casa de España, 1940, 154 pp.

Veinte años de educación en México, Imprenta Universitaria, México, 1941.

Historia de la filosofía en México, Imprenta Universitaria (Biblioteca de Filosofía Mexicana, Vol. X), 1943, viii and 186 pp.

Filosofía de la vida artística, Espasa-Calpe (Colección Austral, No. 974), Buenos Aires-México, 1950, 145 pp.

II. Articles and Prologues

"Antonio Caso, ensayos críticos y polémicos," *Vida Mexicana,* November 6, 1922.

"Las ideas en México después de la Reforma," *México Moderno,* III (1923), pp. 35–38.

"José Torres," *El Universal,* January, 1925.

"El sueño de Diego," *Los Contemporáneos* (México), VI (1930), pp. 113–126.

"El sueño de México," *Los Contemporáneos* (México), VII (1930), pp. 103–118.

"La cultura criolla," *Los Contemporáneos* (México), XI (1931), pp. 61–82.

"La personalidad de Hostos," *Letras de México,* II (February, 1939), p. 1.

"La preocupación de la muerte," *Letras de México,* II (October, 1939).

"Concepto de la filosofía según Bergson," *Homenaje a Bergson,* Centro de Estudios Filosóficos de La Facultad de Filosofía y Letras, Universidad Nacional Autónoma de México, 1941.

"Notas de estética," *Filosofía y Letras* (México), No. 1 (1941), pp. 43–49.

"El movimiento científico en la Nueva España," *Filosofía y Letras* (México), III (April-June, 1942), No. 6, pp. 169–178.

"Veinte años de pintura en México," *Revista Ars* (Buenos Aires), I (January, 1942), pp. 3–14.

—(Reproduced in *Cultura en México* (Boletín de la Comisión Mexicana de Cooperación Intelectual), I (July-Dec., 1942), pp. 23–26.)

"Hubo filosofía entre los antiguos mexicanos," *Cuadernos Americanos,* I (March–April, 1942), No. 2, pp. 132–145.

[José Enrique Rodó] *Rodó,* Selection and prologue by Samuel

Ramos, Ediciones de la Secretaría de Educación Pública, México, 1943, xxvii and 171 pp.

[Plato] *Apología*, Prologue by Samuel Ramos, Ediciones de la Secretaría de Educación Pública, México, 1944.

"Influencia de la cultura francesa en México," *Cuadernos Americanos*, III (September–October, 1944), No. 5, pp. 140–153.

"Las tendencias actuales de la filosofía en México," *Intellectual Trends in Latin America*, University of Texas Institute of Latin American Studies, 1945, pp. 44–54; English translation, pp. 55–65.

"Antonio Caso, filósofo romántico," *Filosofía y Letras* (México,) XI (April–June, 1946), No. 22, pp. 179–196.

"La filosofía de Antonio Caso," *Cuadernos Americanos*, V (May–June, 1946), No. 3, pp. 122–133.

"La personalidad artística," *Filosofía y Letras* (México), XII (October–December, 1946), No. 24, pp. 251–266.

"Responsabilidad e irresponsabilidad de los filósofos," *Cuadernos Americanos*, VII (November–December, 1948), pp. 83–97.

[Diego Rivera] *Acuarelas, 1935–1945*, Text by Samuel Ramos, The Studio Publications (Colección Frieda Kahlo), New York, 1948, 18 pp., 20 plates, 4 color reproductions.

"La cultura y el hombre de México," *Filosofía y Letras* (México), XVIII (October–December, 1949), No. 36, pp. 175–185.

"En torno a las ideas sobre el mexicano," *Cuadernos Americanos*, X (May–June, 1951), No. 3, pp. 103–114—(Reproduced as Appendix II of the present volume).

[Justino Fernández] *Coatlicue: Estética del arte indígena antiguo*, Prologue by Samuel Ramos, Centro de Estudios Filosóficos (Ediciones del IV Centenario de la Universidad Nacional, No. 15), 1954; 2nd edition, Instituto de Investigaciones Estéticas (Colección "Estudios de Arte y Estetica," No. 3), Universidad Nacional Autónoma de México, 1959.

"Relación entre la filosofía y la ciencia," *Seminario de Problemas Científicos y Filosóficos*, Cuaderno 1, Universidad Nacional Autónoma de México, 1955, 8 pp.

[Antonio Caso] *Antonio Caso, Antología filosófica*, Prologue by Samuel Ramos, Biblioteca del Estudiante Universitario, No. 80, Universidad Nacional Autónoma de México, 1957, xl and 265 pp.

"Concepto y método de la metafísica de Heidegger," *Revista Mexicana de Filosofía* (1958), No. 1, pp. 51–59.

"La estética de R. G. Collingwood," *Dianoia*, Anuario de Filosofía, Fondo de Cultura Económica, México, V (1959), No. 5.

III. TRANSLATIONS

Plotinus, *Enéadas*, Universidad Nacional Autónoma de México, 1923.

Aldous Huxley, "El banquete de Tillotson," *México Moderno*, III (1923), pp. 209–223.

Benedetto Croce, *Breviario de estética*, Editorial Cultura, México, 1925.

Wilhelm Dilthey, *La esencia de la filosofía*, Filosofía y Letras, México, 1944.

John Dewey, *El arte como experiencia*, Prologue and translation by Samuel Ramos, Fondo de Cultura Económica, México-Buenos Aires, 1949, xxi and 315 pp.

Bertrand Russell, *Religión y ciencia*, Breviarios del Fondo de Cultura Económica, No. 55, México, 1951.

INDEX